Van Cleef & Arpels

Van Cleef & Arpels

SYLVIE RAULET

Illustrations compiled by
SYLVIE RAULET and FRANÇOIS CANAVY

Photographs by
JACQUES BOULAY

RIZZOLI
NEW YORK

For J.B.

First published in the United States of America in 1987 by
Rizzoli International Publications, Inc.
597 Fifth Avenue, New York, NY 10017

Copyright © 1986 Editions du Regard, Paris

Library of Congress Cataloging-in-Publication Data

Raulet, Sylvie.
    Van Cleef & Arpels.

    Includes index.
    1. Van Cleef & Arpels.   2. Jewelers—France—
Biography.   3. Jewelry—France—History—20th century.
I. Title.   II. Title: Van Cleef and Arpels.
NK7398.V36R3 1987   739.27′092′2   [B]   86–42721
ISBN 0–8478–0754–1

Set in Janson type by Rainsford Type, Ridgefield, CT
Printed and bound at Imprimerie Attinger, Neuchatel, Switzerland

Contents

The Hôtel de Germain-Boffrand, 22 Place Vendôme, where the House of Van Cleef &
Arpels opened in June 1906.

INTRODUCTION

"There are some signatures which one knows one can trust" might translate the motto "*Il est des signatures auxquelles on tient*" which has for years appeared in Van Cleef & Arpels' catalogues and advertisements. It was inspired by an incident with a loyal client, who had been alarmed to receive a ring which had been enlarged in the House's workshops and from which the signature had completely disappeared. The omission was instantly remedied. In a sense, this book is the history of that signature, for the latter has become a symbol which, since the turn of the century, has embodied jewelry in all its aspects. Often plagiarized—but this in itself is proof of the originality of a style which has, over the years, retained its own identity in spite of changing fashions—Van Cleef & Arpels' creations have never ceased to amaze us with their uncompromising line, their inventiveness, their classicism, but also their boldness and sometimes even their extravagance. Recording them in these pages, and retracing their history and their development, we are inevitably recounting the history of the jeweler's art in the twentieth century.

Portrait of a
Dynasty of Jewelers

About halfway through the nineteenth century, an able young lapidary craftsman started a business in Amsterdam. Charles Van Cleef had a flair for recutting gemstones whose flaws diminished their value. The principal jewelers of Amsterdam flocked to him, drawn by his reputation. Very soon he realized that possibilities for expansion in that city were limited and would not satisfy his ambitions for long. At that time, reports of France's wealth under Napoleon III, and accounts of Parisian social events—the endless succession of balls and receptions glittering with the jewelry worn by the most elegant society women—were spreading abroad. In 1867, unaware of the imminent fall of the Empire, Charles Van Cleef decided to set himself up in Paris. Here, in a very short time, he acquired a considerable reputation and he met and married his wife who, on 13 December 1873, bore him a son, Alfred.

Throughout his schooldays at the Lycée Charlemagne, Alfred filled his notebooks with sketches of jewelry; after matriculating, encouraged by his father, he started an apprenticeship in the workshops of Messrs. David et Grosgeat. He stayed there only six years, preferring to take up the profession of salesman rather than work in a jewelry workshop. In 1898, he married his cousin, Estelle, the daughter of Léon Arpels, a dealer in precious stones, and went into partnership with his two brothers-in-law, Charles and Julien Arpels. The three of them founded a jewelry business. The youngest Arpels brother, Louis, did not join the firm until shortly before the First World War. The traditional family business of diamond-dealing, which had been handed down from father to son, thus came to an end.

The firm was first located in an unpretentious office on an upper floor at 34 rue Drouot, but their business flourished; their skills were complementary and their reputation went from strength to strength. The limited space of their initial premises proved constricting, so they moved to 22 Place Vendôme, the shrine of Parisian elegance to which, since the opening of the Ritz Hotel in 1898, wealthy foreigners had flocked.

Alfred Van Cleef (1873–1938), one of the House's founders, at Monte Carlo.

And so it was at the turn of the century, while Art Nouveau practiced its magic and displayed its sinuous curves, that the young firm of Van Cleef & Arpels was launched in the world of *haute joaillerie*. It was begun in what turned out to be the justified hope of forging an empire that would hold its own against even the most well-established jewelers. On 16 June 1906, the new premises were formally inaugurated and responsibilities were divided up according to the partners' respective aptitudes. Alfred Van Cleef (1873–1938), aesthete and strategist, took charge of administration and production; Charles Arpels (1880–1951), a gifted salesman, ensured that courtesy, charm and discretion reigned supreme in the shop; Julien Arpels (1884–1964), thanks to a solid theoretical knowledge and incomparable intuition, excelled in choosing precious stones. He was responsible for negotiations with the most important dealers and traveled the world over in search of new treasures. Estelle was entrusted with the firm's accounts. It was she, at the beginning of the thirties, who was at the bottom of the word *minaudière*, because—as her brothers used to say—no one could *minauder* ("simper" is the closest English equivalent) in society with such charm and spontaneity as she.

Without a doubt the moment was well chosen for the launching of such a venture. Since the *Exposition Universelle* in 1900, the Russian aristocracy, whose prodigality was legendary, had flocked to France. Wealthy American women would not consider renewing their wardrobes and selecting their jewelry anywhere but in Paris and wealthy sons had not yet had time to waste their family's fortunes. It was a time of luxury and eccentricity when you could admire the diamond-studded garters at Maxim's and when dancing girls might be thrown a bouquet of violets in which rubies were concealed.

In a few months, Van Cleef & Arpels had achieved an overwhelming success. They were obliged to employ a salesman, then two, then a female assistant and by 1912 they had no fewer than fourteen members of staff. It was at this time that the youngest Arpels brother, Louis (1886–1976), chose to join the family business. He

Charles (1880–1951) and Julien Arpels (1884–1964), two of the House's founders.

proved to have a talent for selling and he was to instruct a whole new generation of salesmen.

The first attempts to expand the Paris-based business were a response to the ritual migrations of the cosmopolitan élite to such seaside resorts and watering places as Deauville, Biarritz, Vichy and the Riviera. The firm was obliged to follow its customers and, as early as 1906, the first branch was opened at Dinard. Even today one can see Van Cleef & Arpels' name outlined in mosaic on the pavement. In 1910, in Nice, the little shop at 8 rue Masséna (now in the Avenue de Verdun) was opened, some two years before the firm established itself in Deauville in the rue Gontaut-Biron, near the Casino and the Hotel Normandy, recently built by Eugène Cornuché and François André.

Success at Deauville was not long in coming. Robert de Beauplan has given us the following list of regular visitors: "Grand Dukes of Slav origin and Indian Rajahs, Spanish marquises and Corned Beef kings, great ladies and ladies of the *demi-monde*, crowned heads and crooks, financiers about whom one hesitated to predict whether one day they would be worthy members of the *Légion d'honneur* or guests of the Santé prison, politicians in favor, fashionable painters touting for American women who wanted to have their portraits painted . . . " Among the royal guests, the most popular was certainly Alphonse XIII, King of Spain, who seemed to devote more time to Deauville's festivities than to affairs of state. Pierre Roudil, society columnist for the newspaper *Gil Blas*, tells a rather disconcerting anecdote about him. One day, quite by chance, the king met his mistress, the singer Geneviève Vix, and suggested that she accompany him to Van Cleef & Arpels to choose a piece of jewelry. It is easy to imagine Miss Vix's confusion and how she hesitated, when confronted by so many splendid jewels. At last she made her choice. The king thanked her for her help and said, quite naturally, that he had been looking for a gift for the queen on her saint's day. Geneviève Vix could hardly wait for the king to leave before giving way to her vexation.

Louis Arpels (1886–1976), one of the House's founders.

The staff of Van Cleef & Arpels in 1923, in front of Alfred Van Cleef's house, later called "La Minaudière."

The most popular of the watering places was Vichy. In 1913, at 6 rue du Président Wilson, the firm established a shop which was to be open every year during the high season. Unfortunately, the declaration of war in 1914 interrupted any further expansion projects. Charles was called into the English army as an interpreter, Louis rejoined his artillery regiment and Alfred Van Cleef, rejected on grounds of bad health, managed the firm's affairs on his own for four years. His wife, Estelle, offered her services as a nurse and left for the front and a hospital founded by Baroness Rothschild; she was awarded the *Légion d'honneur* and the *Croix de Guerre* for her devoted service. Emile Puissant (1888–1926), a young lieutenant in the Mountain Light Infantry, was among the wounded men for whom she cared. While on leave, he met Renée, the daughter of Estelle and Alfred Van Cleef. After their marriage, Emile, invalided out because of war wounds, assumed responsibility for the administration of the

House. His career was unfortunately cut short when he killed himself at the wheel of his Bugatti in February 1926, as he was entering Monte Carlo, a victim to his passion for racing-cars.

With the return of peace, the firm concentrated on two objectives: consolidating the success of the shop in the Place Vendôme, which was enlarged in 1920, and pursuing its policy of expansion in France and abroad. The wealthy members of cosmopolitan high society were discovering the pleasures of sea and sun and the House decided, in 1921, to open two branches in Cannes: "La Brise," at 24 promenade de la Croisette, open in winter (it was finally closed in December 1963), and the summer shop, at No. 69. This was closed down in August 1963, a new shop at No. 61 having been opened the previous year.

Unhappily, the firm's first attempt to establish itself in Lyons, at No. 47 rue de la République, ended in failure, and the shop closed down on 5 September 1921. It was only a slight hitch for this young firm whose success was confirmed at every important exhibition in which it participated: the *Exposition d'Art Français* in New York in 1924, the *Exposition Internationale des Arts Décoratifs* in Paris in 1925, where it was awarded an important prize, and the *Exposition de Joaillerie et d'Orfèvrerie* at the Musée Galliera in 1929.

During the twenties, Emile Puissant introduced an innovation which was quite unexpected in the realm of jewelry and to which the rival jewelry establishments did not take kindly: every year, between the 10th and 31st of December, a sale took place. Between seven hundred and one thousand items were described in great detail in a catalogue and very reasonably priced. One can easily imagine the interminable queue outside the shop in the Place Vendôme and the vexation of certain rival establishments who went so far as to call these events "rummage sales." This venture was reintroduced in the fifties in November, solely for the benefit of regular clients.

After her husband's death, Renée Puissant (1897–1942) offered to take over the position of artistic director. She excelled in this and—until her accidental death in 1942—became over the years a

Renée Puissant photographed at the Longchamp races in 1935. Artistic director of Van Cleef & Arpels from 1926 to 1942, she collaborated closely with the designer René-Sim Lacaze and had a great influence over the style of creations made between the two World Wars.

designer of international repute who contributed to a large extent to the firm's prestige.

Freely admitting that she could not draw, she nevertheless ensured that the products of her exuberant imagination were faithfully transferred onto paper by draftsmen such as René-Sim Lacaze, a gifted draftsman and designer who was attached to the House between 1922 and 1939. The two of them formed a brilliant partnership, with their complementary talents and aesthetic affinities. All design sketches were submitted to Renée Puissant who, after scrutinizing them, suggested any modifications that would be necessary to ensure a perfect execution.

Endowed with a very strong personality, she also had charm, elegance and beauty reinforced by vitality and an attractive, if sometimes disconcerting, spontaneity. She took a passionate interest in her work, but this did not prevent her from taking pleasure in society. On all occasions she represented Van Cleef & Arpels in a brilliant and captivating manner.

After the First World War, Van Cleef & Arpels' American clientèle presented advantages which could not be ignored: unlimited means and a great loyalty to the House. The firm decided to set up a branch in New York and rented a 'corner' in a colleague's premises, opening their doors on Thursday the 24th of October, 1929, the day of the Wall Street crash. Some years later this enterprise was abandoned, a casualty of the economic situation.

In spite of the repercussions of the financial crisis in France at the beginning of the thirties, the firm sustained its expansion efforts. After mature reflection, they decided, together with some twenty other jewelry-makers, to participate in the 1931 *Exposition Coloniale*, held in the Bois de Vincennes, in an attempt to exorcise the economic depression which was devastating the luxury industries. Accordingly, a number of the pieces exhibited displayed an exotic inspiration, and ivory took its place beside sumptuous pieces set with precious stones. Incompetent organization of the exhibition provoked a number of protests from the jewelers. Henri Clouzot reported in *Les Arts Précieux à l'Exposition Coloniale* that their stands had been relegated to the back of the Palais Metropolitain, "in an out-of-the-way room, next to the boilers and central heating installations, [in] a gallery with a low ceiling and no architectural merit, at most suitable for an exhibition of domestic utensils."

As an antidote to the prevailing gloom, Van Cleef & Arpels had recourse to advertising: every evening an image was projected on the drop curtain at the Folies Bergères, and, on the Champs-Elysées opposite Fouquet's, an enormous poster (at least fifteen meters long), designed by Jean-Gabriel Domergue, glorified the *Minaudière*. Every year, New Year's greetings were addressed to the most faithful clients on handpainted parchment, in gothic lettering. In 1928 concern with advertising led them to organize a graphic art competition in the revue, *La Renaissance des Arts et des Industries de Luxe*: competitors were asked to devise an image, an outline, a theme which might be used on the House stationery, which would perfectly evoke Van Cleef & Arpels. More than a thousand projects were submitted on such themes as the Vendôme column, hands laden with gemstones or pearls, an elephant good-luck charm, the Chinese god of riches, and the thieving magpie. From all these images, the judges selected a geometric design by Robert Couaillier as most characteristic of the age.

The great industrial wealth concentrated in the north of France encouraged the House to open a branch at the Carlton Hotel in Lille on 1 December 1930; in 1933 it was transferred to the Royal Hotel, while a new shop was established in the Cercle de l'Industrie building in Roubaix. Important transactions occurred only very rarely and Van Cleef & Arpels gave their preference to the seaside resort of Le Touquet Paris-Plage where their shop, in the Avenue Verger, was opened in 1927 and did not close down until the eve of the Second World War.

In spite of the economic and financial depression, the beginning of the thirties was one of the firm's most successful periods. The creation of the "*Minaudière*," an exquisite box of chased gold set with precious stones which incorporated, ingeniously fitted into the small space, all the essential accessories an elegant woman could not do without, was just one of the House's achievements. Furthermore, the perfecting of *serti invisible*, a process exclusive to the House whereby the metal settings of precious stones were virtually hidden, was an invention of major importance which revolutionized traditional *haute joaillerie* techniques, bringing Van Cleef & Arpels considerable prestige.

From 1935 on, brooches, cuff links, corsage ornaments, earrings, bracelets, necklaces and boxes, all unique pieces, were made in *serti invisible* and fetched enormous prices. Some required the perfect matching up of several hundred gemstones which were cut to within a hundredth of a millimeter and which, in the end result, resembled a dazzling marquetry of color and light.

In 1932 the firm decided to enlarge the shop in the Place Vendôme and it attained its present day dimensions; premises which had formerly been those of the prestigious Maison Lalique at no. 24 were annexed. The directors also became aware of the need to establish an exclusive collaboration with a workshop.

Choice fell on Alfred Langlois, a watch- and clock-case-maker of repute who specialized in making vanity cases and who had, for several years, worked principally for Van Cleef & Arpels but also for Janesich, Lacloche, Ostertag, Boucheron and Mauboussin, among others. An exclusive contract was signed on 1 July 1933. Alfred Langlois, at that time supervising fifteen craftsmen, demanded the utmost skill from his employees. A piece of jewelry would be executed in an atmosphere of concentration. Nothing could disturb the meticulous attention to detail with which designers, model-makers, lapidaries, stone-setters and polishers worked, using tools which had sometimes been made by the craftsmen themselves and were like those that had been used for centuries.

After her father's death in August 1958, Odette Langlois (who had for some time worked alongside him) took over management of the workshop which, since the beginning of the thirties, had been in the rue Saint-Martin and whose staff had recently grown from fifteen to forty in number.

Independently of the connection established with this workshop, Renée Puissant also forged links with some independent jewelry-makers, bringing reciprocal influences into play which were mutually beneficial. Projects initiated outside the House, after having been modified if necessary to conform with the house style, were either carried out in Van Cleef & Arpels' workshops or directly by the makers. Among these, we might mention Strauss-Allard et Meyer, and Frey for vanity cases; Desmares for handbags; Verger for clocks; Rubel, Lenfant, Péry, Mirra, Boisson, Ehret (now Stringer) and Dumont for jewelry; some have since disappeared and others, such as Vassort and Profillet, have taken their place.

The House continued to prosper and on the 24th of December 1935 a new branch opened in the casino at Monte Carlo, inside an upper rotunda, in one corner of the façade overlooking the square. Rapid success obliged it to expand and at the beginning of 1937 the showrooms were enlarged, all the while complying with the restrictions imposed by the Municipality which dictated that the façade of the building (by Garnier) retain its symmetry. More recently, in 1978, a basement room used as a rehearsal room by the Opera chorus was also annexed. The newly refurbished shop was inaugurated with great *éclat*, in the presence of Princess Grace of Monaco.

Despite the difficult economic situation and the imposition of very strict exchange controls abroad, the 1937 *Exposition Universelle* took place in Paris, in an area extending from the Place de la Concorde to the Quai de Passy. Van Cleef & Arpels achieved considerable success, unaware of the misfortune that was to strike the following year with Alfred Van Cleef's death. He had been a founder-member of the company, considered by all to be one of the principal authors of the House's prosperity and dazzling success. Throughout his career he had been able to communicate his enthusiasm and passion for his work to one and all. He had waited until the last years of his life to make a journey round the world, during which every single member of staff received post cards sent from every stop on his itinerary.

His funeral procession, at his express request, made a circuit of the Place Vendôme, bidding it a final farewell, before leaving for Nice in the south of France.

The same ceremony took place in 1964, on the death of his brother-in-law, Julien Arpels, thus establishing a family tradition.

In 1938, on receiving a request from the Egyptian Court that the House should execute the jewelry to be worn at the marriage of Princess Fawzia, daughter of King Fouad and sister of Farouk, to Reza Pahlavi, King of Iran, Jacques Arpels was dispatched to Cairo to supervise the many projects that were planned. All the jewelry intended to be worn by the Princess and her mother, Queen Nazli, and by the entourage of the royal family (tiaras, *parures*, etc.), was to be made in the Paris workshops with precious stones selected from the House's own collection. Dazzled by such splendor, Princess Fawzia was to remain a loyal client of Van Cleef & Arpels and she never failed to visit their showrooms when she visited Paris. In October

King Farouk and Queen Nazli in 1939, at the wedding of Princess Fawzia and the Shah of Iran.

Her Majesty Queen Nazli of Egypt, wearing a diamond tiara, pendant earrings and necklace created in 1939, on the occasion of the marriage of her daughter, Princess Fawzia, and the Shah of Iran.

Princess Fawzia of Egypt, on her wedding day, wearing a diamond tiara, pendant earrings and necklace created by Van Cleef & Arpels.

The Shah of Iran and Princess Fawzia on their wedding day, in 1939.

*Drawing of the necklace worn by Queen Nazli on the wedding day of her daughter,
Princess Fawzia of Egypt.*

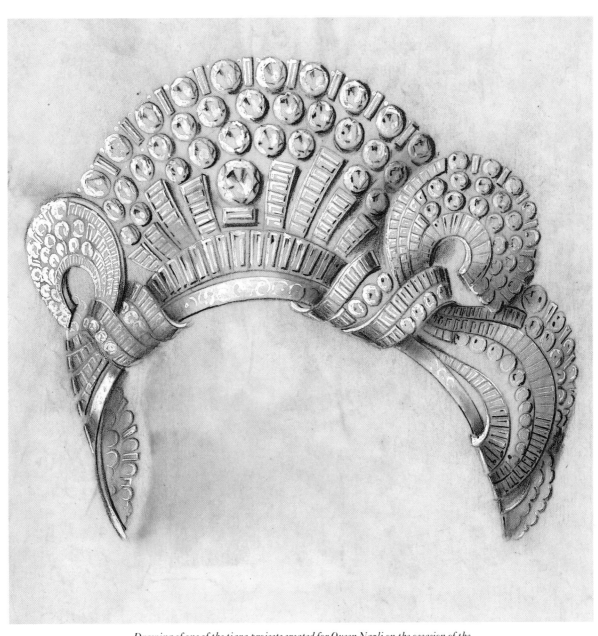

Drawing of one of the tiara projects created for Queen Nazli on the occasion of the marriage of her daughter, Princess Fawzia of Egypt.

1951, she was lent a *parure* for a gala evening at the Opéra; the princess received so much attention from photographers that she simply had to buy it for herself.

After participating in the 1939 New York World's Fair (30 April to 27 October), Louis, Julien and the latter's young son, Claude Arpels, established themselves permanently in New York, determined to exorcise their disaster of 1929. It was a major turning-point in the House's history. Despite cutthroat competition, their success was spectacular and their office, on the 36th floor of Rockefeller Center soon took over from the shop in the Place Vendôme which was paralyzed by the war. In fact, from 1940 onwards, trading in gold was prohibited by the Bank of France, which required a customer who commissioned an article in gold to provide 100% of the metal required; this, however, was a lower percentage than that required for platinum, which was 135%. When gold and platinum were melted down, the State reserved to itself the right of preempting 20% of the total weight.

Most of the male members of staff were called into the army; the importing of precious stones was brought to a halt. The House was consequently reduced, more often than not, to remaking pieces of jewelry in the contemporary style.

The exceptionally favourable reception which Van Cleef & Arpels met with in New York encouraged the House to open a branch at Palm Beach on the 4th of October, 1940, followed, in 1941, by the enlargement of their premises in Rockefeller Center which they left in 1942 to move into a new shop at 744 Fifth Avenue (the New York equivalent to Paris' rue de la Paix), which in turn was enlarged in October 1950. In accordance with a plan devised by Louis Arpels and Princes Foucaud and Philibert de Bourbon, two of the House's senior salesmen, a third branch was opened at the end of 1947 in Dallas (closed down in 1958), followed by one in Caracas in 1957 (closed down in 1975), and finally one in Beverley Hills, on millionaires' hill, in 1969.

The New York shop enjoyed a special status: it was, in effect,

Mrs. Louis Arpels in 1934; this photograph appeared in the Officiel de la Couture *of that year.*

the only one to offer models that were especially created for the American clientele. Close collaboration between Paris and New York meant that Claude Arpels could order *haute joaillerie* models from the Place Vendôme, while at the same time offering pieces that had been executed on the spot by workshops serving Van Cleef & Arpels/New York exclusively: Le Henaff, under the direction of a former Parisian *chef d'atelier* and the Arpels Manufactory, which was in California. To encourage young jewelry designer-makers, every year Claude Arpels invested a considerable sum towards the prize awarded by the Fashion Institute of Technology to the winner of a competition.

After the opening of the first American branch, the two inseparable brothers, Julien and Louis, shared their time between Paris and New York. Louis had the ideal qualities for establishing special relationships with the clientele and certain regular clients in particular; Marlene Dietrich and Maurice Chevalier became personal friends. A keen fisherman, a fine horseman and the owner of a small racing stable, he assiduously frequented race courses in the company of his wife, who was declared to be one of the ten best-dressed women in the world by a panel of American judges; her beauty was celebrated in the society columns and in this respect she competed with her brothers' and nephews' wives who were all extolled for their grace and elegance, ideal ambassadresses for Van Cleef & Ar-

The Arpels family in 1954, on the occasion of President Vincent Auriol's official visit to the United States. From left to right: Mrs. Jacques Arpels, Mr. Jacques Arpels, Mrs. Julien Arpels, Mr. Julien Arpels, Mrs. Claude Arpels, Mr. Claude Arpels, Mr. Louis Arpels, Mrs. Pierre Arpels, Mr. Pierre Arpels.

pels' luxurious image. Faithful to his office in the Place Vendôme, Louis Arpels spent more than eighty years there, alternating, as occasion demanded, between sternness and a good-mannered familiarity, to his employees' delight. As for his brother, Julien, he was as precise and even-tempered as Louis was charming and imaginative, this contrast in their characters serving only to draw them closer together throughout their lives. Obliged to scour the world to further their business interests, they met up again with pleasure at their homes at Mougins and Germigny.

Around 1935, the second generation entered on the scene. Julien Arpels' three sons, Claude (born in 1911), Jacques (born in 1914) and Pierre (1919–1980), were initiated into the business alongside their elders. Claude, a graduate of Harvard and the Ecole des Hautes Etudes Commerciales, made his début in the business in 1936, and after spending some time in Paris and Cannes, moved permanently to New York in 1939. Passionately interested in literature, poetry and music, it was he whom Balanchine approached in 1975 to devise the outline for a ballet on the theme of precious stones, which was performed by the New York City Ballet at the New York State Theater at Lincoln Center, and subsequently at the Théâtre des Champs-Elysées.

In 1945, with the return of peace, the Parisian House resumed its activities with an enthusiasm which was all the greater for the years of trial. It took part in an exhibition organized at the Pavillon de Marsan on the theme "the little theater of fashion," in which dolls, dressed by the great couturiers, Schiaparelli among them, were adorned with jewelry by the principal jewelers. Jacques and Pierre joined the older generation. Jacques took up his position in the Place Vendôme at the age of twenty in 1934, where he acquired a thorough background to the House's different departments before specializing in precious stones, a field in which he soon acquired an international reputation. A shrewd and demanding director, guided by an enduring enthusiasm which sustained his unflagging determination, he demanded from his collaborators the same discipline and precision

Marlene Dietrich at the Bal des Petits Lits Blancs, in 1938, at Cannes. Photograph by R. Schall.

Balanchine and Pierre Arpels with Suzanne Farrell between them in the Place Vendôme showrooms, in 1976, on the occasion of the opening of a ballet put on at the Champs-Elysées theater on the theme of precious stones, inspired by Claude Arpels.

33

that he imposed on himself throughout his life. As he was fond of saying, he wanted things to be precise "to a hundredth of a millimeter, to a hundredth of a carat." A skilled horseman, golfer and Alpine skier, an art and nature lover, he was more capable than anyone of appreciating the perfume "First de Van Cleef & Arpels," which was created in 1976.

As for Pierre, he joined the company at the end of the Second World War. His elegance, courtesy and charm won all hearts and he was an ideal spokesman for the House in all matters concerning public relations.

However, he also liked to exercise his virtuosity in the realm of jewelry and created "puzzle," multiple-function jewelry. He was unquestionably the principal sportsman of his family; he not only rode, skied and went hang-gliding (he was the 1963 world record-holder), etc., but also took part in aquatic sports, of which he was particularly fond, such as wind-surfing which he discovered towards the end of his life. After his disappearance in 1980, Jacques Arpels, as a memorial to his brother, set up an annual trophy for wind-surfing (this competition is classed as a national event).

With the end of the war, the Vichy branch could move back into its former premises at 23 rue du Parc, but as this resort's popularity declined, the shop was only opened during the season when

Jacques Arpels with his father, Julien, on his right and his uncle, Louis, on his left.

34

Pierre Arpels (1919–1980) photographed in December 1975.

people customarily visited the hot springs in 1946, 1950, and 1952, before being permanently closed down in 1953, when the public turned its attention to the Cap d'Antibes where a new branch was opened at the Hotel du Cap from July 1949 to October 1957.

During these years the House's first priority was to win over a new clientele and to this end all sorts of imaginative efforts were made. In one instance, an open letter of invitation to a "special private sale" of jewelry was inserted in each copy of *Le Monde*. In collaboration with the great couturiers, Van Cleef & Arpels allowed their own creations to be modelled by mannequins wearing clothes designed by Jacques Fath, Balmain, Jean Patou and Marcel Rochas at fashion parades. At the end of the forties, on the occasion of an important fashion parade of Rochas designs at Saint-Moritz, arranged for the 28th of December, Jacques Arpels was detained by Swiss customs officials who insisted on placing in bond the jewelry he had brought with him. He was forced to send the entire collection back to Paris and had to go on to Saint-Moritz empty-handed. However, the incident had a happy if unforeseen outcome. Three of Van Cleef & Arpels clients, who were guests at the hotel, offered to lend their finest jewelry (Van Cleef & Arpels creations, of course) for the fashion show, a unique event in the history of fashion.

Throughout the fifties, Van Cleef & Arpels participated in all the prestigious celebrations organized in Paris. In June 1950, to celebrate the Place Vendôme's two hundred and fiftieth anniversary, their windows were the cynosure of all eyes. Each window illustrated a theme dear to French hearts of the eighteenth century: the Literary Salons, the Arts and the Muses, the Love of Nature, the Glory of the French Army. The following year, the bimillenniary of the city of Paris, saw the House participating in a lavish evening organized at the Musée de la France d'Outremer on the 17th of December, at which President Vincent Auriol was present, together with three hundred members of the United Nations and principal figures of literary and artistic Paris. After the symphonic suite conducted by Henri Sauget and played by the Concerts Lamoureux, and one act operas celebrating the glory of Paris, came the climax of the spectacle: mannequins modelled the latest in formal evening wear designed by Pierre Balmain, Jean Dessès, Jacques Heim and Jacques Estérel, sparkling with Van Cleef & Arpels' most splendid *parures* (at that time valued at nine million francs).

Fully aware of the irreversible changes that had occurred in a society which was still evolving, the House decided, in 1954, to set up the first "Boutique" opened by a premier jeweler, in premises adjacent to the main shop. In this way the House could, on the one hand, broaden its clientèle and, on the other, offer models more suitable for young women who usually could not wear more elaborate jewelry. According to Jacques Arpels, the "Boutique" was to be the antechamber to the *haute joaillerie* shop.

This venture was repeated in New York in 1957. The success of these creations, made in several copies, was immediate and lasting, reflecting the loyalty of the French clientèle, who made up about seventy percent of the total, as opposed to thirty percent in the *haute*

Claude Arpels.

joaillerie showroom only a few meters away. It should be noted, however, that even before the "Boutique" was set up, Van Cleef & Arpels had been making items of costume jewelry, heralding the "Boutique's" collections of such popular pieces as the "Chat Noir" or "Petit Lion" clips or the "Philippine" rings.

But it was among captains of industry, film stars and crowned heads that the House achieved its most brilliant successes. In 1956, the Principality of Monaco requested the House to take charge of Princess Grace's wedding present which was to include, in particular, a *parure*—necklace, bracelet and earrings—in diamonds and pearls, Prince Rainier's own present to his bride, and a bracelet comprising five rows of diamonds which was commissioned by the National and Municipal Council. Some months later, Prince Rainier conferred on Van Cleef & Arpels the title of "Official Purveyor to the Principality." The lavish celebrations marking the Prince's marriage afforded the House the opportunity to serve other notable guests. For example, Tina Onassis chose a necklace of eight rubies, with a total weight of 80 carats, set with diamonds. (In 1978, on Princess Caroline's wedding day, Princess Grace was to wear a tiara set with seventeen pear-shaped diamonds, navette diamonds and brilliants, yet another of the House's creations).

Since the sixties, Van Cleef & Arpels have organized numerous exhibitions all over the world, prestigious occasions which have taken place in palaces, in the presence of eminent celebrities. It was at this time, moreover, that the House decided to participate regularly in the Biennale des Antiquaires, which was generally mounted at the Grand Palais in Paris. For a long time, Pierre Arpels was the driving force behind these occasions. After long years of experience in the Place Vendôme dealing with the clientèle, Yvan Le Tourneur, who had managed the Geneva branch (set up in 1960) since 1966, assisted him in this capacity. After Pierre Arpels' death, he took complete charge of these exhibitions, whose schedule was always carefully arranged so as to fit in with the seasonal migrations of high society.

Grace Kelly wearing the necklace and earrings of pearls and diamonds given to her by His Majesty Prince Rainier of Monaco to celebrate their engagement, New York, 1955.

The first took place in Gstaad, at the end of December 1966 and has been repeated every year at the same time, in addition to an exhibition in February. At the same time, the collections are also presented at the rival resort of Saint-Moritz. Since 1977, on the 27th of December every year, a lavish dinner is given at Gstaad, to which forty celebrities are invited (foreigners as well as French guests are present). Yvan Le Tourneur has an indelible memory of the tea party to which he was invited every New Year's day by Nina Kandinsky so that she could admire and select the jewelry she would buy that year. Her passion for emeralds was so great that she even called her chalet "Esmerelda." She would offer her guests caviar and vodka but Yvan Le Tourneur and his wife, feeling themselves unequal to alcohol in the middle of the afternoon, used to empty their glasses into the azaleas.

Elizabeth Taylor never failed to visit Van Cleef & Arpels on her visits to Switzerland; her whims were so imperious that she would think nothing of telephoning Yvan Le Tourneur and asking him to drop everything and bring her pieces of jewelry that she wanted immediately. Such an occasion occurred when she was on location at Cortina d'Ampezzo and a pair of earrings had to be delivered to her as a matter of urgency.

The travel schedule for the collections unfolded with ritual regularity; Gstaad in December and February, Saint-Moritz in February, Hong Kong in May, Monte Carlo and Marbella in August, Lugano in October. During the seventies, when the price of a barrel of black gold (oil) was rising ever higher, Mr. Le Tourneur visited the Persian Gulf three times a year in order to gratify the slightest whims of the numerous wives of the various Emirs.

In 1971, four years after the Empress Farah's crown had been created, Iran celebrated the 2,500th anniversary of the Persian Empire in the majestic setting of Persepolis. It was here that the Oeuvre des Petits Lits Blancs decided to celebrate its fiftieth anniversary. To commemorate this, Van Cleef & Arpels created a symbolic pendant depicting a winged lion—the emblem of the Persian Empire—whose delicate detail and coloring recalled Persian miniatures. This unique piece was presented to the Empress, the guest of honour at this gala. A few copies in gold were offered for sale by subscription in aid of the "Farah Pahlavi" and "Petits Lits Blancs" charities.

It should be stressed here that Van Cleef & Arpels, fully aware of belonging to a privileged class, have always been and are still in the habit of making such donations towards funds for the underprivileged. While making no attempt to draw up an exhaustive list, we might mention here some of the principal beneficiaries: the Red Cross, the "Petits Lits Blancs," the Fédération des Evadés de Guerre, and the Anti-Cancer League.

Although, since 1906, the firm has always offered an exclusive range of watches, the setting up of the "Boutique des Heures" marked a new stage in its history. A caprice of Pierre Arpels' was at the core of this venture. In 1949, wishing to possess a unique watch, he designed one for himself. Taken aback by the enthusiasm of his friends and clients, he decided to produce the model commercially under the name "P.A. 49." This watch became the point of departure for a whole range of watches for both men and women which resulted, in 1972, in the opening of the new shop.

In the same year, Japan, for a long time protected by very strict regulations governing the import of crude or refined gold, eventually decided to open its frontiers to jewelers from abroad. No sooner had they been informed, than Van Cleef & Arpels threw themselves enthusiastically into the conquest of this new world and signed a franchise agreement, negotiated by Pierre Arpels with one of the most important business conglomerates, Seibu Department Stores. The president of Seibu, Mr. Tsutsumi Seiji, a figure of international repute, a talented businessman and well known poet, worked actively to promote his commercial empire and the worldwide diffusion of all forms of artistic expression. This project, based on reciprocal loyalty and exclusivity, spread a network across Japan of fourteen outlets, which were of two distinct types. On the one hand, small shops were set up which were devoted exclusively to selling

Philippe Arpels in 1983.

Van Cleef & Arpels' creations, exact replicas of the shop in the Place Vendôme, all situated inside vast department stores next to celebrated French Houses such as Hermès, Vuitton, Scherrer and Yves Saint-Laurent. On the other hand, there were entirely independent shops like the one in Marunouchi, Tokyo, a few meters from Ginza, the district where business and the luxury trades are centered. All the collections presented were executed exclusively in Parisian or New York workshops, and the Japanese customers, if they had a predilection initially for the "Boutique" collections, soon were drawn to the *haute joaillerie*. It should be noted that commissions of pieces in the Japanese style were very rare, it being more "chic" to wear jewelry that was "made in Paris." Temporary exhibitions of the latest creations, organized in premier hotels, were so successful that Van Cleef & Arpels decided to try to set up more all over the country. The Japanese travelers who assiduously frequent many of the branches of Van Cleef & Arpels in the West testify to the prestige of French jewelry.

The only jeweler to have branches in Monte Carlo, Cannes, Geneva, New York, Palm Beach, and Beverley Hills, the House has also granted franchises to several boutiques organized on specific lines, in collaboration with reputable local firms. The arrangement of these ventures punctuated the House's activities throughout the seventies and eighties. A list of these outlets gives an idea of the House's extraordinarily wide field of activities: Sao Paolo (1973–1978), Zurich (in the large Grieder department store, November 1976–May 1983), Milan (in the Corso Vittorio Emmanuele, opened in May 1979), Kuwait (opened in February 1980), Hong Kong (in the Peninsular Hotel and the Gloucester Tower, opened in May 1980), Singapore (1981–1984), Lugano and Madrid (opened in 1981), Brus-

Jacques Arpels and his daughter, Dominique Hourtoulle, in 1983, studying a piece of jewelry especially created by Van Cleef & Arpels for the Maharanee of Baroda.

sels (in the Galerie Louise, opened in December 1982), London (at 153 New Bond Street, opened in September 1983), Rome (opened in November 1984).

In the middle of the seventies, Jacques Arpels' two children and his brother Pierre's daughter joined the House: Philippe Arpels specialized in the study of gemstones, dealings with the clientèle and public relations; his sister, Dominique Hourtoulle, took an active part in the creation of *haute joaillerie* and Boutique models as well as public relations; Caroline Daumen collaborated in the publicity department. The perpetuation of family management is assured.

Place Vendôme

Maria Callas in the blue salon at the Place Vendôme in the early sixties, trying on an exceptional parure: a pear-shaped diamond of 49.13 carats in a very subtle cognac color forms the central motif of a collerette with matching earrings embellished with two pear-shaped diamonds from Sierra Leone with a total weight of 50.61 carats, evidently cut from the same stone.

Since its inception, the House of Van Cleef & Arpels has always observed an absolute discretion as to the identity of its clients. Only anecdotes that lie outside the seal of secrecy can therefore be related here, and the list of names reads like the international edition of "Gotha."

The Begum Aga Khan, about 1955.

Here are just some of the House's eminent clients: the Prince of Nepal; King Farouk and the Court of Egypt; Prince Ibrahim; the Duke of Westminster; the Duchess de Talleyrand; the Princess de Faucigny-Lucinge; the Marquise de Bonni-Picenard; Lady Deterding; Lady Granard; Lady Maclean; Sir Edmund Findlay; Mme. Martinez de Hoz; Mrs. Fellows; King Peter II of Yugoslavia; Prince Rainier and Princess Grace of Monaco; the Aga Khan and the Begum; Queen Frederica of Greece and her son Constantine; Queen Sirikit of Thailand; the Court of Iran . . . and the list goes on.

Since time immemorial, gemstones and pearls have exerted an almost magical attraction. A very wealthy client, Countess Costantini, was so fascinated by pink pearls that, over a period of twenty years, she amassed an extraordinary collection. She would buy them singly and insisted they were perfect; at Van Cleef & Arpels she found the most rare specimens.

At the turn of the century, a number of Indian maharajahs fell in love with Europe and with France in particular. They all knew each other and even organized polo matches at Deauville in summer! They did not hesitate to have their ancestral treasures transformed—and even enriched—in the European fashion. Notable among them were the maharajahs of Indore, Hyderabad, Jaipur and Gwalior and the Maharajah of Morvi who bought a green, cushion-shaped diamond of about nine carats, one of the finest Jacques Arpels had ever seen. As for the Maharajah of Kapurthala, his admiration for France led him, in 1909, to build a palace on the model of Versailles!

The Maharanee of Baroda, who was known to be mad about pearls and precious stones, had a cupboard whose many drawers

were crammed with pearls in every conceivable shade. In her apartments, scattered here and there, jade and onyx vessels overflowed with precious stones. Julien and Jacques Arpels were called in to value her extraordinary collection (more than three hundred pieces of jewelry) and the task took several days to complete. Some of the pieces dated back to the Napoleonic era and were the spoils of war of one of the Maharanee's ancestors.

In the thirties, Madame Snauwaert tried to outbid Julien Arpels for a gorgeous triple row of exquisite pearls which was being

The Prince of Nepal in the early thirties.

The Maharajah of Baroda and Jacques Arpels on a sleigh ride, January 1948.

48

Her Highness Seeta Devi, Maharanee of Baroda, holding her son, Princie. She was the instigator of some of the House's most fabulous creations, recalling the splendor of Indian jewelry of the past. She had an absolute passion for very fine emeralds and rubies and, most of all, for pearls, 1948.

*The Duke and Duchess of
Windsor at the Château de
Candé, in 1937, on their
wedding day. The Duchess is
wearing a dress by Mainbocher
with a clip in sapphires and
brilliants especially created by
Van Cleef & Arpels.*

Collerette *in diamonds mounted on platinum—the upper part could be detached and
worn on its own as a choker—created in 1964 for Her Majesty Queen Sirikit of
Thailand, using a Thai motif, on the occasion of the marriage of King Constantine of
Greece and Princess Anne-Marie of Denmark.*

*Lily Pons, in 1951, wearing a
"Ballerina" necklace in gold
and brilliants.*

*The Begum Aga Khan and Mrs. Louis Arpels at a ball given in the early fifties.
Photograph by André Ostier.*

auctioned at the Hôtel Drouot by the étude Ader, which had been entrusted with disposing of the jewelry belonging to one of the Dolly Sisters. Madame Snauwaert had to bow out but could not resist, the very next day, begging Julien to sell her the necklace.

During these same years, the Prince of Wales was a loyal client of the House and remained so after he became Edward VIII. On 3 June 1937, love triumphed over reasons of state and the Duke of Windsor married Wallis Simpson at the Château de Candé. She chose to wear, with a pale blue satin dress designed by Mainbocher (her favorite New York couturier), a Van Cleef & Arpels clip comprising eleven faceted sapphires, baguette diamonds and brilliants arranged in the geometric style characteristic of the period.

No less impressive is the list of great financiers and industrialists, as, for example: the Mellons; the Vanderbilts; the Kennedys; the Opels; Baron Empain; the building contractor Mathis; George Blumenthal, the American banker and collector; but also German bankers: Manheimer, Bram, Cassel; the Patinos; the Thyssens; Barbara Hutton and her aunt, Mrs. Donahue; Mrs. Merriweather Post; Mrs. Henry Ford II; Florence J. Gould; the Goulandrises; the

Gloria Swanson in 1950, at the Knickerbocker Ball.

Hair ornament forming a net of diamonds, worn by Elizabeth Taylor at the "Proust" ball given in 1972 by Baron and Baroness Guy de Rothschild.

A pensive Elizabeth Taylor at the "Proust" ball given in 1972 by Baron and Baroness Guy de Rothschild. Photograph by Cecil Beaton.

Douglas family; the Onassises; the Béghins; Madame Veil-Picard (the owner of Pernod) who never failed to visit Van Cleef & Arpels a few days after her rival, Madame de Rivaud, had done so; Louis and Eddy Baron, the proprietors of Craven cigarettes; Madame Sapêne, the wife of the newspaper proprietor of *Le Matin* and an opera singer in her own right under the name Claudia Vitrix.

Amongst these famous names we should not forget the stars of screen and stage: Madeleine Carroll, to whom Claude Arpels sold her first sapphire necklace, the color of the stones being ideally suited to complement her deep blue eyes; Lily Pons, who sang at the Metropolitan Opera for twenty years and for whom Claude Arpels designed all the jewelry which she wore on stage in *Lakmé*; Joan Fontaine; Danielle Darrieux; Michèle Morgan; Gloria Swanson; Maria Callas; Marlene Dietrich, a personal friend of Louis Arpels; and Paulette Godard (then Charlie Chaplin's wife) who was so impatient by nature that one day she summoned one of the House's salesmen to wait on her at the hairdresser so that she could choose a piece of jewelry. Elizabeth Taylor created a great stir at the "Proust" ball given by Baron and Baroness Guy de Rothschild in 1972; she wore a gorgeous hair ornament, virtually a net of diamonds which was worn over a chignon created by the famous hairdresser, Alexandre de Paris.

Credit must be given here to certain salesmen whose great skill, and often patience, have contributed to the prosperity and prestige of the House. They have known how to satisfy the desires of a clientèle whose behavior might, at the least, be termed eccentric. One salesman, for example, was pacing up and down the gaming room at the Cannes casino one Christmas evening, when suddenly he became aware that someone was gently but firmly taking him by the arm. He turned round to see a very good client, Baron Johnny Empain. "Old boy, you must do me a small favor. I've forgotten a few presents that I was going to give to some friends . . . and they're coming to dine with me shortly!" The salesman, after having helped the Baron to choose seventeen pieces of jewelry in the shop (not far

Ludmilla Tcherina at a ball, her plaited hairstyle, haloed with brilliants, is spiked with feathers from which jeweled ornaments are suspended, circa 1960.

from the Casino), and wrapped up seventeen little parcels and sealed them, heard midnight strike. "I only have sixteen guests," the Baron said to him, "the seventeenth parcel is for you, with my compliments."

A very distinguished lady, Madame Gallier (her husband was one of the co-founders of the Liquid Air company), wanted to acquire a very fine brilliant, which she intended to give to her grandson's fiancée. Accordingly, she selected three very beautiful rings and asked the salesman to be good enough to bring them to her the next day at about midday, so that the young girl might make her choice. Confident of a satisfactory outcome to this sale, the salesman took himself off to a charming little private hotel in the rue de la Faisanderie. To his great surprise, he discovered, comfortably ensconced in one of the rooms, three gentlemen whom he knew by sight: salesmen from Cartier, Chaumet and Boucheron! At Madame Gallier's request, each in turn entered an adjoining room, where our salesman was the second to enter. Before dismissing him, Madame Gallier merely said, "I will let you know my decision tomorrow morning." Very disappointed, he was about to withdraw when he suddenly had a brilliant inspiration: he deliberately "forgot" his gloves on an armchair. After taking his leave, he went into a café opposite, sat down and watched his rivals leave, one after another. Shortly afterwards, he called again, excusing himself to Madame Gallier and saying that he merely wanted to retrieve his gloves. Once alone with her, it was child's play for him to use his powers as a salesman to convince her . . . and, of course, he won the day.

One of the most important qualities a jewelry salesman must possess is intuition, the ability to assess a client's personality at once, to know instinctively how to go about meeting him.

What had become of Sir Edmund Findlay, a loyal client who had come regularly to make purchases at the Place Vendôme? He had not been seen there for over two years so it was decided to reestablish contact with him by despatching a salesman, armed with an attaché case stuffed with pieces of jewelry, to Sir Edmund's Paris ad-

Sophia Loren wearing ear drops of emeralds and brilliants, circa 1966.

Joan Fontaine wearing a flexible necklace to which are attached three snowflake ornaments of baguette diamonds and brilliants, with matching earrings, circa 1948.

dress. There, he was told that the latter was in London. Accordingly, he was instructed to set off for London the very next day. At that time the cross-channel journey was no simple matter, it involved taking a train, then a boat, then another train to London, where our salesman arrived in the early afternoon. Here he was told by Sir Edmund's butler, "I'm sorry but Sir Edmund has left for his Edinburgh residence." The same evening, the salesman took the night train to Edinburgh. He barely had time to make himself presentable at a hotel in this city before repairing to Sir Edmund's house. "I'm sorry, but Sir Edmund has already left for London." He caught the train once again. In London he made a second visit and was told, "I'm sorry, but Sir Edmund has already left for Paris." Our unfortunate salesman was obliged to retrace his steps, London, Dover, Calais, Paris! Somewhat harassed, he returned to the Place Vendôme where his colleagues greeted him with the dreadful news: "Just guess who came in here yesterday? Sir Edmund Findlay."

Jacqueline Kennedy wearing diamond and platinum clips in her hair.

Van Cleef & Arpels have always believed in luck and they have had cause to do so. They have also on occasion brought good luck to their customers. One day, one of the House's secretaries received a call from a Mrs. G., a very important client of Van Cleef & Arpels New York. She was frantic, she had arrived in Paris that very morning and believed that, in a taxi taking her to her hotel, she had lost a superb ruby of more than ten carats which her husband had given her. It should be explained that Mrs. G. had had a special mount made for her ruby; the stone was set in a detachable bezel (a little gold "basket") and by adjusting a tiny screw, the precious little "basket" could be removed and the stone attached to a clip or a ring, as it had been at the moment when Mrs. G. had lost it. She had suddenly become aware that the ring on her finger had only its two lateral diamonds, and at the center of the ring there was only a hole.

The secretary and Mrs. G. appealed at once to the police, to the Lost Property office, to the taxi companies—all in vain. However, so as to have exact particulars of the stone, the secretary asked for all information concerning the ruby and its mount to be dispatched from

New York. She received it the next day and was showing it to the resident expert when the latter, with a look of utter amazement, said, "Wait a minute! I'll just get something out of the safe." Shortly afterwards he returned with a ruby set in a gold bezel. Mrs. G. had entrusted the secretary with the empty mount and they feverishly attempted to put the bezel in the center of the ring. It fitted perfectly! There was no doubt about it, this was indeed Mrs. G's ruby. But how on earth had it turned up in Van Cleef & Arpels' safe? Quite simply, another of the House's clients, who happened to be staying at the same hotel as Mrs. G., had found it on the pavement in front of the entrance to the hotel. Her first thought, on seeing the stone (whose considerable value she guessed) set in its gold bezel, was to take it to Van Cleef & Arpels.

Catherine Deneuve, in 1980, in François Truffaut's film Le dernier métro, *wearing the "Belle Hélène" necklace comprising a serpent chain of polished gold and brilliants, created in 1946.*

Were it not for the restrictions of professional secrecy, the House's salesmen could compile a whole volume of amusing anecdotes; however, some of these can be included here because, over the years, they have become part of the House's history. The Marquis Boni de Castellane, for example, on his frequent visits, used always to stand back to allow his dog, whom he treated with great formality, to pass first. Then there was the German banker, always accompanied by two gorgeous women—a blonde and a brunette—who insisted on bathing in Evian water at the Hotel Meurice. Then there was the Polish financier who commissioned a special *minaudière* encrusted with diamonds for his beloved, on which he wished to engrave her surname, "Biebele," with his own hand; Annabella also commissioned a *minaudière*, engraved with images from her most important performances (*Hôtel du Nord*, *Les Nuits moscovites*, etc.). Mrs. Gilbert Miller, daughter of the New York banker and collector, was given a brooch in *serti invisible* by her father, an exact replica of Goya's "Little Boy in Red" which she adored. The picture belonged to her father and she was very disappointed when she learned that he had bequeathed it to the Metropolitan Museum of Art.

Clip designed in 1962 by Chagall in the Van Cleef & Arpels studio at the Place Vendôme, for his wife's birthday. This unique cock was made of gold, brilliants, topazes, sapphires—one of these being a cabochon—and calibré emeralds.

In 1962, wishing to give his wife a unique piece of jewelry designed by himself as a birthday present, Chagall chose Van Cleef &

Arpels' workshop in the Place Vendôme as the ideal place to initiate himself into the art of jewelry. He took great pleasure in scrupulously choosing each precious stone that was to embellish the clip which had been designed for this special occasion: a crowned cock in the naive style reminiscent of his paintings.

Van Cleef & Arpels have always followed their trade with a passion and enthusiasm that arouse their clients' admiration. The following story is a good illustration. In the thirties, a very important American banker—a collector of fine stones well known to the House over twenty-odd years—paid a visit to the Place Vendôme showrooms. He asked for the sales manager, with whom he usually dealt, and the latter showed him a magnificent ruby of about twenty carats. More than an hour passed in talk and negotiation but the client had still not made up his mind when Julien Arpels, who had just arrived, asked to be introduced to him. After a conversation lasting no more than five minutes, the client, fired with enthusiasm, bought the ruby from him, asking him how, in so short a time, he had managed to convince him. "It's very simple," Julien Arpels replied. "I myself bought the stone; I also had it recut to make the most of its brilliance; I also devised a mount that would display it to the best advantage. In a sense, this jewel is my child. That is why I can speak so passionately about it and communicate to you my love of fine stones and perfect craftsmanship."

At the same time as they produce their own creations, Van Cleef & Arpels also carry out *commandes speciales* (special commissions), all of which are engraved with the initials "C. S." next to their signature. One of these special commissions, and perhaps the most extraordinary, deserves to be described in detail.

On 26 October 1967, the young queen Farah, wife of His Imperial Majesty Mahommed-Reza, Shah Pahlavi, was to be crowned the first Empress of Iran. Never, throughout the history of this empire, had such an honor been accorded to a queen. The pomp of the coronation ceremony, which was to rival the legendary ceremonies of ancient Persia, required exceptional preparations, and the crea-

Elizabeth Taylor, at a soirée at the Paris Opéra in the sixties, wearing a tiara and earrings of pear-shaped and navette diamonds and brilliants.

Romy Schneider in 1982, wearing a necklace and pendant of oval faceted Burmese sapphires and brilliants.

tion of the Empress's crown was one of the most extraordinary.

In October 1966, Pierre Arpels received an official visit from the Iranian Ambassador to France and the Governor of the Central Bank of Iran, who asked him to submit some suggestions. Thirty designs were sent off, via the Embassy, to Teheran. Shortly afterwards, Van Cleef & Arpels learned that, out of fifty designs—other important jewelers had also been approached—only three had been selected, two of which bore their signature. In Iran, the imperial crowns were not the sovereign's property, but formed part of the National Treasury which was administrated by a committee comprising the most important dignitaries of the Empire. No decision could be made without consulting them. One of the two projects signed by Van Cleef & Arpels won the support of the committee and the queen. The enterprise was a daring and even perilous one because, although the crown was to be made in Paris, the precious stones were in Iran and on no account could they leave the Central Bank, whose doors gave access to the chamber which housed the Crown Jewels. Faced with these unexpected difficulties, Pierre Arpels decided to travel there to assess the situation on the spot, quite unaware, at this stage, that another twenty-four journeys lay before him. He was fascinated and dazzled by the marvels assembled in this veritable museum: the famous Daria-I-Nour diamond of 182 carats; the Nader-Shah *aigrette*, one of the finest pieces remaining of the Sefevid treasures; the crown of the Kians; the Nasser-ed-Dine Shah terrestrial globe, encrusted with 51,000 precious stones; and the most recent Pahlavi crown, created in 1924 from a selection of the finest stones in the Crown Jewels, and which His Majesty the Shah of Iran was to wear on the day of the Coronation. Pierre Arpels spent whole days in the underground chambers of the Central Bank selecting stones which would adorn the crown of the first Empress of Iran: a 150 carat emerald of matchless splendor was to be the heart of the piece.

Another three long days were necessary to find the ideal stones to surround the emerald. Pierre Arpels began to realize that modifi-

Empress Farah Pahlavi on 26 October 1967, the day of her coronation.

cations would have to be made, and that, gradually, the whole design would have to be rethought.

An initial *canevas* (a two-dimensional drawing, taking no account of volume or perspective) was prepared, on which was marked the location of each numbered stone: 1,541 stones in all, of which 1,469 were diamonds, 36 rubies, 36 emeralds and 105 pearls. Furthermore, most of these pearls, which were pear-shaped, had already been mounted in other pieces, but in different ways. It was therefore necessary to make a precise note of the location of each hole, its exact diameter and depth so that the grey gold "stems" that were to support them would fit exactly.

In the Paris workshops, different *canevas* followed on the first,

Crown created for the coronation of the Empress Farah, comprising engraved emeralds, pear-shaped and round pearls, rubies and diamonds. The claws are of gold, the mount of platinum.

61

Necklace worn by the Empress Farah on 26 October 1967, the day of her coronation. It consists of a pendant in the form of a hexagonal engraved emerald, four emerald-cut emeralds, four pear-shaped pearls, eleven yellow cushion-cut diamonds and antique-cut diamonds, mounted in platinum and gold.

faithfully reproduced in large blocks of black wax. After ten days of intensely hard work, Pierre Arpels, accompanied by a draftswoman and the head craftsman of one of the workshops, left once more for Teheran with more than sixty kilos of material. The stones that had been selected were placed one by one in the black wax blocks, in the places reserved for them, so as to get an idea of what the ensemble of stones would look like. An impression of each stone was then taken in a special plaster into which metal was subsequently poured which, when hardened, would be an exact replica—accurate to a hundredth of a millimeter—of the shape and volume of the stone. Each of these metal replicas was, in turn, numbered and engraved with a reference mark which would ensure that the stone would fit into its setting at the desired angle. All these delicate operations were carried out in a conference room adjacent to the bank's strong rooms, under the supervision of eight principal court dignitaries.

It took six months of work before the crown could be placed on the queen's head and she marveled at its magnificence and its lightness. It weighed 1,950 grams and had an adjustable band on the inside to allow for a perfect fit.

Other jewels were created for the coronation ceremony: a necklace and a pair of long pendant earrings for Her Imperial Majesty Farah Pahlavi; a *parure*—tiara, necklace, pendant earrings—in emeralds and diamonds for Princess Chahnaz, daughter of Shah Reza Pahlavi's first marriage with Princess Fawzia of Egypt; a necklace and pendant earrings in white and cognac-colored diamonds for Princess Fatimah, the Shah's half-sister; a tiara, a necklace and pendant earrings in diamonds and emeralds for Princess Shams, the Shah's eldest sister; a *parure* in diamonds and rubies for Princess Achraf, the Shah's twin sister; and tiaras with leaf and flower motifs in diamonds and emeralds for the Princesses Farahnaz and Leila, daughters of the Shah and Empress Farah.

In 1977, a sumptuous *parure* was also made for Her Imperial Majesty Farah with floral motifs in gold, brilliants and turquoises.

Tiara with leaf and flower motifs in brilliants with seven round ribbed emeralds, made for Princess Farahnaz, daughter of the Shah and the Empress Farah.

SWORDS FOR ACADEMICIANS

Some of the principal French jewelers have had the privilege of designing and making the swords which are offered to new academicians at a private ceremony by friends, admirers or a committee from their native town. Although belonging to a non-military institution, the members of the various Academies which go to make up the *Institut de France* nevertheless wear a sword at their sides when they wear their black uniforms decorated with green olive branches (designed, so it is said, by the painter, Jacques-Louis David, 1748–1825). The origin of the sword, on the other hand, is totally obscure, no documentation relating to this having been found. The regulation concerning the academicians' uniform, dated 13 May 1801 (23 Floral, Year IX), makes no allusion to it, and it was only towards the end of the First Empire that the sword made its appearance. Each member of the *Académies*—the *Académie Française*, founded in 1635 by Cardinal Richelieu; the *Académie des Inscriptions et Belles Lettres*, dating from 1663; the *Académie des Sciences*, founded in 1666; the *Académie des Sciences Morales et Politique* together with the *Académie des Beaux Arts*, both created by the 1795 Convention—receives this honorary symbol.

The House of Van Cleef & Arpels was selected to execute the sword of Maréchal Juin, who became an academician on 7 May 1953, in the chair of the writer Jean Tharaud. This vermeil sword was protected by a precious sheath of green shagreen; one side of the pommel was decorated with a Moor's head (representing the first Corsican), in tribute to his mother, the other with a sheaf of corn symbolizing the goddess Ceres. On the tang, between two crosses, the seven stars of Maghreb were engraved and the names of his campaigns were inscribed on the hilt: Africa, Corsica and Italy. The hand-guard was embellished with a pair of crossed marshall's batons and an escutcheon representing a cock crowing at daybreak, a symbol chosen by the Marshall to represent the Battle of Italy. The but-

Detail of Marshall Juin's academician's sword, in vermeil with a green sharkskin sheath, 1953.

65

ton depicted the Maghrebin star enclosed by the crescent of North Africa.

Twenty years later, Van Cleef & Arpels created the sword that was to be presented on 24 March 1973 by Jacques Duhamel to Jean-Jacques Gautier, theater critic and writer, received into the Academy in Louis Armand's chair. To symbolize theatrical criticism, Jean-Jacques Gautier chose to have the gold hand-guard decorated with the eye drawn by Claude-Nicolas Ledoux, architect to the king in the eighteenth century, in whose pupil the theater at Besançon is reflected. Beneath the hand-guard, the button is embellished with an ear, to commemorate his first novel, *L'Oreille*, written in 1942. The ear was also a symbol of the critic's duty to listen.

A year later, on 2 May 1974, André Roussin took his place under the *Coupole*. As tradition dictated, the academician's sword which the House of Van Cleef & Arpels executed for him, from a design by the celebrated theater designer Georges Wakhewitch, symbolized both his private life and his career as a writer. At the base of the hilt, mimosa flowers against a background of green stones celebrated Provence; higher up, a crystal ball evoked *La Voyante*, the famous play created by Elvire Popesco; the *Rideau Gris* was wound round the hilt (a souvenir of the company in which André Roussin made his début), set off with the arms of Marseilles, his native city; in the angle of the cross, an ivory egg recalled another play, *Les Oeufs de l'autruche*; at the center of the hilt, in keeping with the rest, the body of a man formed the shaft, an image of the silhouette of *Bobosse*. Finally a gold *Petite Hutte*, symbol of his greatest success, crowned the sword.

Journalist and eminent historian Robert Aron received his academician's sword at a reception in the rooms of the Maison de l'Amérique Latine on 17 April 1975. The hilt, surmounted by a horse's head in engraved gold, recalled his passion for racing and his accomplishments as a fine horseman. On the body of the sword an oval plaque in solid gold is engraved with three Hebrew letters, the first, middle and last letters of the alphabet, signifying truth, an essential requirement of the historian. Below this is a gold plaque adorned

Gouache design for an initial project by Georges Wakhevitch for Andre Roussin's academician's sword, 1974.

with the letter "S," the first initial of a person very dear to him.

Bernard Gavoty, music critic and musician in his own right, entered the *Académie des Beaux Arts* on 9 March 1976, taking the chair previously occupied by Julien Cain. He received his academician's sword from the hands of his illustrious colleague at the *Institute*, the pianist Artur Rubinstein, on 16 February 1977. It was designed by Jacques Lenfant and executed by Van Cleef & Arpels. A gold plume curls round a bundle of organ pipes in silver to form the hilt and from this vine leaves and musical notes spill over. The sword is surmounted by a rock crystal pommel, symbolizing clarity, and the button is embellished with the figure of Calliope, the muse of eloquence and patron of orators.

Marshall Juin in his academician's uniform, 1953.

Advertisement   *designed by Charles Martin, which appeared in the magazine*
Harper's Bazaar in 1930. One of the models is wearing a necklace with drop emeralds,
baguette and trapezoidal diamonds and brilliants, mounted in platinum, with matching
earrings; the other is wearing a necklace in drop and square sapphires, baguette,
trapezoidal and square diamonds and brilliants; a bracelet in cushion-cut sapphire
cabochons and baguette diamonds is on her wrist.

Prestigious
Transactions & Acquisitions

If the jeweler's business consists in creating superb pieces of jewelry, it depends equally on his discovering exceptional precious stones. Accordingly, the House of Van Cleef & Arpels has a vast organization spanning the continents. All over the world, agents indicate the presence of stones from which it will be possible to compose pieces that will be remarkable for their unity, flawlessness and harmony.

While this market seemed inexhaustible thirty years ago, nowadays it may be necessary to wait for months, sometimes years, in order to match stones, that is, assemble stones whose similarity will unify a piece of jewelry. Paris was the scene of the most important transactions. Every day, at the Place Vendôme, Julien and Jacques Arpels would receive the most eminent dealers, such as the diamond specialists Myram Eknayan, Benjamin Asscher and the Rubel brothers; Raphael Esmerian, Nersessian and René Eschwège, specialists in colored gemstones; and the three Rosenthal brothers, the Baron de Lopez and Robert Sachs, all specialists in pearls, as was Jean Rosenthal.

At the beginning of the sixties, economic problems upset this situation and Paris lost ground to New York, London, Geneva and Zurich. Furthermore, mines today no longer produce high quality specimens equivalent to those of past centuries. Thus, in 1976, it was necessary to wait for three years to finish a ruby bracelet because stones of similar color were lacking. The younger generation, incarnated in Philippe Arpels, fears the closure or exhaustion of certain mines which will bring about significant changes in the profession; no longer will it be a matter of discovering new stones, rather of continually dismantling old pieces and devising new pieces from them.

The evaluation of a precious stone is arrived at from a consideration of its purity, its color, its shape, its limpidity and its brilliance, all criteria which require experience, sound theoretical knowledge and flair.

Jacques Arpels, possessing a sharp eye and armed with knowledge passed on to him by his father, trained by daily, meticulous observation of specimens, is one of the most respected individuals in his profession. Two anecdotes will suffice to confirm this judgment. At the beginning of the seventies, a jonquil diamond of 104 carats, the "Deepdene," was put on sale at Christie's in Geneva. Authenticated by numerous gemological experts, it was loaned to and exhibited by the Museum and the Academy of Sciences of Philadelphia, who ranked it on a par with the famous "Tiffany" diamond of 128.51 carats. The "Deepdene" was merely a diamond that had been artificially colored by being bombarded with electrons and only Jacques Arpels could reveal its secret. The "Deepdene," thus nicknamed by its first owner, Mrs. Curtis, was re-sold in 1954 by Harry Winston (a well known New York diamond dealer) to an anonymous buyer. Its career ended in 1971. The same thing occurred at an auction at Christie's in Geneva in 1976 with regard to a jonquil diamond of 40 carats, guaranteed by two certificates of authentication, one of which came from the Swiss Institute for the Study of Precious Stones in Zurich. The stone owed its downfall to Jacques Arpels, who demanded a counter-valuation; this confirmed his doubts and the diamond was withdrawn from the sale.

One can appreciate the immense responsibility that those who deal in precious stones must bear. Julien, Jacques and Claude Arpels have always obtained the collaboration of gemological experts, gifted specialists such as Edmond Mareynat, who occupied this position in Paris between 1931 and 1966, Max Pelegrin who, attached to the firm since 1951, took over from Mareynat, and Véronique Ma'arop, who was preceded by William Norie and Richard Guerringue in New York.

The House of Van Cleef & Arpels, with a few exceptions, only buys cut stones; the business is run exclusively by the family and is consequently independent, entirely self-financing and able, at any moment, to mobilize the necessary funds to enrich its stock.

The composition of the crystal determines the color of a diamond. The most precious white diamonds are totally colorless.

72

Rarer still are colored diamonds, graded as follows according to their rarity: green diamonds (rarely exceeding one carat) with pink diamonds a close second, then blue and yellow diamonds which are found more often. (The difference in price between *extra blanc* or extra white diamonds and colored ones can be five times as much.) The purity of a stone is gauged according to the size of inclusions in the crystal, its sparkle depends on the limpidity of the stone, this being termed the diamond's "water." The ideal form, for Van Cleef & Arpels, is achieved through harmonious proportions determined by the "golden section" for a rectangular or marquise diamond, where the breadth is approximately half the length of the stone.

In India, Golconda, near Hyderabad, was for several centuries unrivaled as a source of diamonds. Its assets had been plundered by 1687 and two centuries were to pass before Erasmus Jacob discovered the first South African diamond in 1866; this country proving to be a prodigious source of mineral wealth. Since 1930, Sierra Leone has undoubtedly produced the most exceptional uncut diamonds. But, beyond Africa, we should not forget Australia, whose mines, worked since the end of the nineteenth century, were augmented in 1976 by the development of the Kimberley district which produces uncut diamonds of high quality but often of small size. The de Beers company exercises a virtual monopoly over the world market, selling to a privileged few uncut diamonds subsequently acquired by diamond dealers or cutters.

A Van Cleef & Arpels catalogue, dating back to the twenties, recalls an incomparable pear-shaped diamond of 60.25 carats imported from Africa at the beginning of the century by Alfred H. Smith and Co. and named the "Prince Edward of York." More recently, in 1959, a pear-shaped, 49.13 carat diamond of a very subtle cognac shade, became, flanked by two pear-shaped diamonds from Sierra Leone (weighing 50.61 carats, evidently cut from a single stone), the central motif of a *collerette*. In 1975, another remarkable *collerette*, named the *Impératrice* (Empress) was created by Van Cleef & Arpels. It was composed of thirteen pear-shaped South African

Pendant comprising a blue brilliant of 7 carats from which a pear-shaped diamond of 44 carats is suspended, from a catalogue of the twenties. Actual size.

diamonds of incomparable purity, patiently collected from sources all over the world; a 21.50 carat diamond formed the central motif and on either side of this, in descending scale, pairs of 22 carat, 11 carat, 9 carat, etc., diamonds were placed, joined by a number of brilliants and navette diamonds with a total weight of 75 carats. A South African diamond of 30.28 carats, an emerald-cut rectangle with cut-off corners, totally colorless and absolutely pure, was mounted in a ring between two small trapezium-cut diamonds; even now, this is considered one of the most extraordinary pieces in the House's collection.

From time to time, diamonds become the focus of interest for speculators, generally because of the public's lack of information, bringing about a flare-up in prices followed by a slump. Van Cleef & Arpels protects itself against these uncontrollable fluctuations by concentrating on the purchase of colored stones. These stones are generally ranked as follows: Burmese ruby, Colombian emerald, diamond and sapphire.

The appreciation of colored precious stones poses a complex problem; the evaluation of the quality of a particular shade remains very subjective. The most important specialists are in agreement when they affirm that a stone's color is more important than its purity; rather a subtle color and some slight flaw than purity and a mediocre color. For Van Cleef & Arpels, an emerald is never more beautiful than when it is warmed with a hint of yellow. In addition, when appraising a stone, it is important to shade it from brilliant sunlight which will always make it appear dazzling.

As far as rubies are concerned, it now seems that the incomparable "pigeon's blood" ruby of Magok (northeast of Mandalay in Burma), whose deep velvety red combines both orange and purple, is beginning to disappear.

Since the nationalization of the mines occurred, bringing about a fall in production, Burmese rubies have virtually disappeared. The authorities, strictly supervising the passage of rubies and sapphires across the frontier, have on occasion preferred flooding the mines to

The "Prince Edward of York," a pear-shaped diamond of 64 carats, suspended from a navette diamond of 25 carats, forming the pendant of a diamond sautoir, *from a catalogue of the twenties. Actual size.*

the unregulated movement of precious stones. Rubies and sapphires being for the most part alluvial in origin, it is merely a matter of turning back the course of a diverted river to flood a mine. Although the most precious gems remain in their country of origin, a few dazzling stones do, from time to time, manage to cross the frontier. These "clean" rubies, that is, stones free from inclusions, with their sumptuous crimson shades, are priceless and only complete familiarity with sources, together with perseverance and good luck, allow the jeweler to match (assemble a number of stones of similar color and shape) several Burmese rubies. Max Pelegrin cites as an example the creation in 1958 of a necklace comprising seven "pigeon's blood" rubies with a total weight of 45 carats and a central stone of 13 carats. All of the stones were of a matchless fruity red color and a perfect

The "Empress" collerette, made in 1975, comprising thirteen pear-shaped South African diamonds: a diamond of 21.50 carats forms the central motif; on either side of this, in descending scale, pairs of diamonds of 22, 11 and 9 carats are arranged, linked by a number of brilliants and navette diamonds with a total weight of 75 carats. Actual size.

homogeneity, and the matching demanded months of patience and forced the experts at Van Cleef & Arpels to dismantle a pair of earring motifs in order to finish the piece. Some years later, an oval "pigeon's blood" ruby of 22.24 carats, whose velvety tones recalled those of a Kashmiri sapphire, was mounted in a ring. More recently, in 1977, an impressive collection of ruby beads from Burma went on sale at Sotheby's in Geneva. Then, the following year, another collection, ideally matched with the first, was discovered in India. The two together made possible the creation of several pieces of jewelry which even today have no equal. But these few examples, it should be stressed, are unique events in the profession.

Siamese rubies are ranked lower than Burmese ones. Though rather less rich in color they nevertheless stand up to comparison with the latter; there follow Ceylon rubies which have a clear raspberry pink color, sometimes heightened with a touch of mauve. Tanzanian rubies or "African rubies" are less rare; their color varies between that of the Burmese to that of the Siamese ruby.

Although emeralds are very often closely associated with the India of the Maharajahs, this country does not in fact possess any significant emerald deposits. In fact, the most ancient mines were in Egypt—Cleopatra's mines—not far from the Red Sea, and they were worked as far back as two thousand years ago. The rarest emeralds were extracted from Colombian mines (the Muzo or El Chivor mines). Their superb color, intense and velvety, neither too blue nor too yellow, haunted the dreams of connoisseurs and speculators. In November 1973, the House of Van Cleef & Arpels acquired, at a Sotheby's sale in Zurich, an "old mine" emerald cabochon (the term "old mine" is given to stones mined in Colombia before the seventeenth century) of 71.43 carats which had served as a maharajah's tunic button. Successive re-cuts eliminated slight peripheral flaws. It was mounted in a pendant, cushion-cut with a weight of 53 carats; an ingenious mechanism released the stone so that it could also adorn a ring. An emerald-cut emerald of 30.35 carats was bought by the House of Van Cleef & Arpels in 1961 in Geneva from an Indian

Parure *composed of Burmese ruby beads, ruby cabochons and diamonds mounted in gold, made at the end of the seventies. Actual size.*

dealer and it became the centerpiece of a necklace comprising twenty-eight brilliants with a total weight of 9.18 carats. Between 1959 and 1961, twenty-two emerald-cut emeralds, perfectly homogeneous, were feverishly sought all over the world in order to create a sumptuous *collerette* set with four hundred and twelve diamonds with a total weight of 70.60 carats.

Another remarkable transaction, in June 1973, was the purchase from a London dealer of an emerald-cut emerald, probably "old mine," of 24.82 carats, mounted in a ring, flanked by two pear-shaped diamonds. This unique stone is even now among the treasures of the Van Cleef & Arpels collection. Brazilian emeralds, sometimes with icy flecks, a little too yellow or too blue but intense in color, play an important role today, competing with those of the Transvaal in South Africa, which have a deep color, sometimes just too dark or flecked with dark hematite inclusions.

Sapphires, the least expensive of precious stones do, nevertheless, when of exceptional quality, reach higher and higher prices. For a long time, the sapphires of Burma and Kashmir reigned supreme. The latter, of a vivid, velvety kingfisher blue, mined since the end of the nineteenth century in the Himalayas at an altitude of five thousand meters, are becoming rarer and rarer, the region having periodically been the scene of territorial conflicts between India and Pakistan. As for Burmese sapphires, in particular those from Magok, their ultramarine blue tends to lose its brilliance at night and to "go to sleep" in electric light. Accordingly, numerous amateurs of gemstones prefer the lighter blue of the Ceylon sapphire—the blue of the cathedral windows at Chartres—which keeps its brilliance at night. Thus, Jacques Arpels prefers a Ceylon ruby of high quality to a guaranteed Kashmiri sapphire of mediocre quality.

Stones extracted from lodes near Ratnapura, in the southwest of the island (which cross the frontier only when officially surtaxed) offer a wide range of shades; pale blue, sky blue, Nattier blue, lavender blue, kingfisher blue, indigo but also yellow, orange, pink mauve, violet, green, black and colorless.

Collerette *made between 1959 and 1961, comprising twenty-two emerald-cut emeralds framed by four hundred and twelve diamonds weighing 70.60 carats. Actual size.*

It is virtually impossible to draw up a comprehensive list of the exceptional sapphires which have been bought by Van Cleef & Arpels; only a few prestigious transactions can be noted here. Three years (1962–1965) passed before it was possible to assemble five Burmese emerald-cut sapphires, acquired from different sources and with a total weight of 90 carats, in order to make a bracelet set with perfectly matched stones which was sold in 1967. In 1969, in Columbo, Jacques Arpels acquired an emerald-cut Ceylon sapphire of 43.16 carats, a quite remarkable, perfectly crystalline, flawless stone; it was mounted in a ring, flanked by two pear-shaped diamonds, a marvel in the House's collection. The following year, a Burmese sapphire, emerald-cut, of 55 carats, a rigorously pure, priceless piece, was offered for sale by a private individual.

In 1979, a *collerette* comprising nine Ceylon sapphires was completed: the search for the stones had required four years of traveling across the world and negotiations with the most important dealers. Arranged symmetrically in descending scale following a restrained and simple design, on either side of a 45 carat sapphire, were paired stones of 27 carats, 24 carats, 15 carats and 11 carats. Van Cleef & Arpels' privileged relations with the most important dealers made possible, in 1980, the creation of a *collerette* as sumptuous as the piece described above, comprising eighteen sapphires of which nine faceted oval stones from Ceylon, weighing 108 carats in all, were re-cut according to the Parisian technique, unequalled the world over, thus endowing each stone with an ideal proportion and brilliance.

These few examples illustrate how a thorough understanding of precious stones must go alongside perseverance and endeavor in order to create the rarest pieces of jewelry.

Eighteen sapphires, including nine oval faceted Ceylon sapphires, with a total weight of 108 carats, set with pear-shaped diamonds and brilliants, make up this exceptional collerette created in 1980. Actual size.

The incomparable sapphire of 114 carats, dubbed the "Blue Princess" or the "Neele Ranee," became, in 1965, at Florence J. Gould's request, the central motif of a necklace, combined with three other important sapphires edged with diamonds and linked with baguette sapphires. Actual size.

INDIA AND PAKISTAN

In the realm of jewelry, the most amazing stories might be told about the pursuit of precious stones, were these not inextricably linked with famous and wealthy people who rely on the jeweler's professional discretion.

In complete secrecy, on information supplied by one of his numerous correspondents scattered all over the world, the jeweler himself departs in the hope of acquiring unique and sometimes legendary stones. Those who are familiar with the infinitely precarious and delicate context of such enterprises can easily imagine the tenacity, steadfastness and self-control which are required for such transactions, and also the emotion tinged with pride when a happy result has been achieved.

Claude Arpels must certainly have been in a state close to exaltation when, in 1956, he acquired the "Neela Ranee" (also called the "Blue Princess") from a Bombay dealer, this being an incomparable sapphire of 114 carats, and also when he had the privilege, the same year, of meeting the Maharajah Sahib Bahadur of Rewa, who wished to dispose of certain stones. Conforming with the custom which forbade a maharajah to enter into direct negotiations with a prospective buyer, Claude Arpels asked a British Colonel to act as intermediary.

From the moment they arrived, the Prince's family and advisors offered them a hospitality whose lavishness and refinement were worthy of the most extraordinary travelers' tales of the nineteenth century. From the choice dishes to the sweetness of the music and the beauty of the dancing girls, everything seemed to have been calculated to whet their curiosity, but they were obliged to wait in their apartments until the following day before they were presented to the Maharajah.

A white tiger which had prowled around for two nights, was captured at twilight as it was trying to enter one of the little palaces. It was here that the Maharajah conducted his guests so that they could admire the captive tiger, the pride of his State, as well as a myriad of jewels which the visitors discovered in a detour leading from a path, arranged in the middle of a grove, crowning a shrub or pinned onto a flower.

Dazzled, Claude Arpels made his choice before returning to his apartments. After a night which was presumably spent in feverish expectation, his intermediary explained to him that he would have to wait until the Maharajah had consulted his astrologer and if the indications were favorable, he would be given a sign.

He returned to Delhi and a week passed before two emissaries arrived at the hotel, bearing a casket containing the jewels that had been selected. Among these was a fantastic cabochon emerald of more than 100 carats; two plastron necklaces of the kind worn by maharajahs on rare occasions, one comprising fifty-five emeralds set in a lattice of diamonds and pearls, from which hung an emerald of exceptional size, and the other a lattice of white diamonds embellished, in the middle, by a pink diamond, extremely rare in India; a "Mauratan" necklace tiara comprising eight stones—emerald, ruby, blue sapphire, yellow sapphire, cat's eye, topaz, coral and diamond—and a single pearl, representing the nine planets of the Indian system of good or bad omen, which Hindu princes wear to protect themselves from harmful influences; a collection of bangles in enamel set with precious stones, depicting dragon or elephant heads and of flexible bracelets intended to adorn the forearm. This collection of jewels was shown to a privileged few at the Plaza Hotel in New York in March 1956.

In the meantime, Claude Arpels had paid a visit to the Maharajah of Jamnagar who possessed a priceless collection of emeralds. In Lunawada he had acquired one of the most sumptuous diamond necklaces he had ever seen and, in New Delhi, some pearls of high quality. As for the oval sapphire, the "Blue Princess" (insured for a hundred thousand dollars), a stone whose brilliant deep blue did not alter in artificial light nor in the most penetrating sunlight, it became, at the request of Florence J. Gould who bought it in 1965, the central motif of a necklace, surrounded by three other sumptuous sapphires flanked with diamonds and linked with baguette sapphires. After her death, this necklace went into the auction sale which disposed of her fabulous collection on 11 April 1984, at Christie's in New York; the necklace, which the experts had thought might fetch eight hundred thousand dollars, was finally knocked down at one million, three hundred and twenty thousand dollars.

Claude and Pierre Arpels on a trip to India in the fifties, always on the look-out for new acquisitions.

THE "BLUE HEART"

The "Blue Heart," a blue diamond of 30.82 carats, suspended from a triangular blue diamond of 3.81 carats surrounded by white brilliants and a pink pear-shaped diamond of 2.05 carats. Actual size.

Blue diamonds are virtually impossible to find. Generally, they are grey-blue, steel-blue or a blue verging on green, but rarely a pure blue which can equal the finest sapphires, their color being closer to that of Ceylon sapphires and the aquamarine of Tongafeno.

The "Blue Heart," a diamond of 30.82 carats, is unquestionably one of the most beautiful diamonds of this kind. In addition to its absolute purity and incomparable brilliance, its blue color, intensely deep, has a mellowness accentuated by its brilliance, so that it is preferred to the "Hope," another famous blue diamond that supposedly brings bad luck to its owner.

The origins of the "Blue Heart" are shrouded in mystery, but it is known that during the last century it belonged to a nobleman who was obliged to part with it, having wasted his fortune for the love of a woman. Cut into a heart-shape by Eknayan and mounted in a corsage ornament set with a triangular diamond and round-, navette- and pear-shaped diamonds in *sertis muguet* (lily-of-the-valley setting), it was bought by Mrs. Unzue from Cartier in 1911.

In 1953, the House of Van Cleef & Arpels acquired it and sold it the same year to a German baron before buying it back in 1960. It was sold once again to Harry Winston who had it mounted in a ring in 1964 before selling it to Mrs. Merriweather Post, who bequeathed it to the Smithsonian Institution in Washington.

The "Blue Heart" made a sensational appearance, worn by Zizi Jeanmaire, at a ball given in the Orangerie at Versailles in aid of cancer research on 16 June 1953. This time it hung from a necklace of diamonds, which were all of great purity, mounted on gold and platinum settings so delicate that the metal was invisible. The pendant comprised a triangular blue diamond of 3.81 carats surrounded by white brilliants, a pink pear-shaped diamond of 2.05 carats, itself embellished with small brilliants, elongated by two marquise-cut brilliants from which, mounted on gold and surrounded by brilliants, the "Blue Heart" was suspended.

THE PINK DIAMOND OR "PRINCIE" DIAMOND

The sale of the thirty-nine millionaires; thus the auction sale that took place at Sotheby's in March 1960 was nicknamed by the English press.

There is no important sale anywhere in the world that is not attended by an eminent representative of the House of Van Cleef & Arpels. This time it was Jacques Arpels' great joy to carry off, under the noses of his rivals, the magnificent "pink diamond," a stone of 34.64 carats, unique, comparable with the very beautiful pink diamond belonging to Queen Elizabeth II of England, whose weight is only 23.60 carats.

The mystery which surrounds certain legendary precious stones was at its most impenetrable with regard to the "pink diamond." At the request of its owner, discretion characterized the entry in Sotheby's catalogue. Even so, the laconic phrase "the property of a gentleman," in accordance with proverbial English understatement, did not prevent rumors in knowledgeable circles that the "gentleman" was none other than the Nizam of Hyderabad, the owner of the Golconda mines. Golconda, the capital of the state of Hyderabad, in the south of India, was completely destroyed by the conquering Mongolians at the end of the seventeenth century. Only a ruined fortress remains from this period.

The "Princie" diamond, a pink diamond of 34.64 carats. Actual size.

The "pink diamond," for centuries part of the fabulous state treasure, was, in accordance with tradition, handed down from generation to generation to the first male heir. After the sale, it took its place on cinema sets and was immortalized by Zizi Jeanmaire in a scene from the ballet *La Croqueuse de diamants* (the diamond-eater), directed by Terence Young.

On 5 April 1960, in order to satisfy the curiosity of a rich, cosmopolitan society, a reception was given at the Place Vendôme, during which the "pink diamond" was accorded the nickname "Princie diamond," as a tribute to the young Maharajah of Baroda, called "Princie" by his friends.

THE "MAZARIN"

The "Mazarin" (a 30.58 carat emerald-cut diamond, its cut dating from the beginning of the century), acquired by Jacques Arpels on 11 December 1964 at a Sotheby's auction in London, still bears traces of the cushion-cut, a rectangle with rounded corners, which it was given by Parisian lapidaries in the seventeenth century on the instructions of Cardinal Mazarin. It was one of the twelve largest diamonds in the royal crown which Mazarin entrusted to diamond-cutters so that the stones might be re-cut according to the method of Louis de Berquem who, in 1475, invented the faceted cut for diamonds in the workshops of his native town, Bruges, before moving to Paris. These diamonds were called the "twelve Mazarins" in tribute to this initiative.

Once again, the most important jewelers in the world gathered in 1964 to vie for this exceptional stone. This unique diamond was sold for an equally exceptional price for an unmounted stone at public auction, reaching the sum of seventy thousand pounds or nine hundred and sixty thousand francs at that time.

The "Mazarin," an emerald-cut diamond of 30.58 carats. Actual size.

THE "THIBAW"

The "Thibaw," an incomparable ruby of 26.13 carats, named after King Thibaw of Burma who reigned at the end of the last century, for a while the property of J. P. Morgan, was bought by Cartier from the banker's daughter. In 1937, Cartier New York resold it to Mrs. Horace Dodge (then Mrs. Dillman) for one hundred and fifteen thousand dollars. It reappeared by chance at an auction at Christie's in Geneva, where Van Cleef & Arpels acquired it on 27 May 1971.

This stone was so valuable that a replica was made in order to study the possibilities of recutting it to eliminate on one side a silk and a slight cavity. The cushion shape was retained with a slight loss and a remarkable result was achieved: an exceptional stone of 24.82 carats which was mounted in a ring and sold to a wealthy collector in 1976.

The "Thibaw," an incomparable ruby of 26.13 carats, acquired by Van Cleef & Arpels in 1971 at an auction at Christie's in Geneva. Actual size.

THE "WALSKA BRIOLETTE"

Like the "Walska Heart," the "Walska Briolette," an impressive yellow, pear-shaped diamond, belonged to the famous thirties diva, Ganna Walska, who was Polish by birth and married Mr. Harold McCormick, son of the Chicago Reaper King. She appeared on stage in Chicago for some years. It was at an auction at Sotheby Parke-Bernet in New York in 1971 that Van Cleef & Arpels carried off the "Walska Briolette," while the "Walska Heart" went to another collection. The former diamond, suspended from the beak of a bird of gold, set with white diamonds, emeralds, and blue and yellow sapphires, was bought in 1972 by a wealthy American industrialist.

The "Walska Briolette," a yellow pear-shaped diamond of 95 carats. Actual size.

BARBARA HUTTON'S TIARAS

To say that Barbara Hutton was mad about jewelry is an understatement. From the moment she awoke, her first care was to select the jewels that she would wear and she would change them at whim, throughout the day, until the small hours. When she tired of certain settings, she would have them changed and modified. She was one of the people who set the fashion for gold mounts, a fashion which has practically superseded platinum mounts today.

Among the finest jewels in her collection, she had a tiara which could also be worn as a necklace. The seven historic emeralds of which it was composed were none other than those which had belonged to the Grand Duchess Vladimir, and had been bought by Mrs. Hutton from Cartier at the beginning of the thirties for over a million dollars. At that time she had asked Cartier London to devise a *parure* for her comprising a necklace, earrings and a ring. The necklace consisted of a heavy chain in the style of the thirties from which, as the central motif, hung an emerald of 100 carats. After the Second World War, Barbara Hutton, tired of her *sautoir*, asked Cartier to make it into a piece of jewelry in the oriental style which could be worn either as a necklace or a tiara. Van Cleef & Arpels seized the unique opportunity, in November 1965, to acquire this tiara. Con-

Necklace tiara bought, in November 1965, by Van Cleef & Arpels from Barbara Hutton. It was made at her request by Cartier after the Second World War, using seven historic emeralds which had belonged to the Grand Duchess Vladimir.

sidering its exorbitant value, Van Cleef & Arpels could not hope to resell it and accordingly they were obliged to dismantle it and divide up the emeralds which were then used in several pieces of jewelry: the central 100 carat emerald, recut in cushion-cut to a stone of 89.48 carats, embellished a pendant, two others became the central motifs of two *collerettes*, two were mounted in earrings and the remaining two in rings. All these jewels were sold to very wealthy foreign clients.

Two years later, Van Cleef & Arpels created a tiara for Barbara

Comprising pear-shaped and navette diamonds and brilliants, this tiara was especially made for Barbara Hutton by Van Cleef & Arpels in 1967.

Hutton comprising six pear-shaped diamonds of 54.82, 21.49, 10.95, 10.67, 4.04 and 3.90 carats respectively, eight pear-shaped diamonds together weighing 7 carats, thirty-six navette diamonds with a total weight of 32.39 carats and one hundred and twenty-seven brilliants weighing 42.84 carats. She was so fond of this tiara that Pierre Arpels, visiting her in her suite in a Parisian palace on a certain occasion when she was indisposed, was surprised to see her wearing this incomparable jewel in bed.

THE RUSSIAN TIARA AND MARY OF
SERBIA'S *SAUTOIR*

Obsessed with emeralds, Queen Mary of Serbia, daughter of King Ferdinand I of Rumania and wife of Alexander I of Serbia, had bought a Russian tiara (*kokoshnik*)—one of the legendary treasures of the Romanov dynasty—composed of cabochon emeralds and diamonds, created in the first half of the nineteenth century.

During the twenties, to have a piece that would form a set with this tiara, the Queen entrusted Cartier with the making of a fabulous *sautoir* consisting of eighteen emeralds from the Serbian crown jewels, a very rare piece which was worn by Alexandra of Greece and Denmark, the wife of the Queen's son, Peter II of Yugoslavia, on her wedding day.

In May 1949, Peter II of Yugoslavia sold the tiara and *sautoir* to Van Cleef & Arpels New York. When the transaction had been completed, Van Cleef & Arpels dismantled the *sautoir*; as for the tiara, it became one of the supreme pieces in their private collection.

A unique piece in Van Cleef & Arpels' private collection, this kokoshnik comprising cabochon emeralds and diamonds was bought by Van Cleef & Arpels from King Peter II of Yugoslavia in 1949.

THE "LIBERTY NECKLACE"

There are always legends attached to antique jewelry of great value. This gorgeous emerald necklace, acquired by Van Cleef & Arpels in 1925, is no exception. Its legend has a basis of truth and throws light on a moment of Franco-American history, being one of a number of fantastic stories which surround the memory of Benjamin Franklin. When, in September 1777, Philadelphia was captured, there was some anxiety about the fate of Tadeus Kosciuszko, a chivalrous Pole who, like La Fayette, had hastened to America to defend the cause of Liberty. The gallant Kosciuszko, adulated and fêted at the Court of Louis XVI, had won many hearts including that of a Countess, herself of Polish origin, who was celebrated for her beauty. One evening, as she was going to a masked ball, she was told that Philadelphia had been taken. Overwhelmed with despair, she ordered her coachman to take her immediately to Benjamin Franklin's house at Passy. Taken aback by this masked nocturnal apparition, he comforted her as best he could, affirming that rumors of Kosciuszko's being in peril had no foundation. The countess, in joyful gratitude, wishing to add her support to the American cause which, at that time, seemed more hopeless than ever, took off her emerald necklace and earrings and gave them to Franklin to help his cause: "Here," she said; "there are thirteen square emeralds and thirteen pear-shaped emeralds, two for each of the thirteen colonies. I beg you, accept these jewels in the name of Liberty." Franklin entrusted French bankers with the "Liberty Necklace," as he had dubbed it, but subsequently, in the feverish turmoil of the Revolution, all trace of it disappeared.

In 1850, the necklace mysteriously reappeared, perfectly intact, at the Mont de Piété and years passed without anyone coming, armed with the pawn-ticket, to reclaim it. Comprising thirty-nine faceted emeralds, either pear-shaped or square, surrounded by antique brilliants, it was accompanied by a pair of pendant earrings, each one comprising two square faceted emeralds, two small square faceted emeralds, and two important briolette emeralds flanked with diamonds cut in the antique fashion. In contrast to certain *parures* of this period which might be accused of a certain clumsiness, the gold and silver mount of this piece was very fine and displayed these emeralds, which are of perfect quality, to great advantage, enhancing their rare color, a green at once deep and velvety.

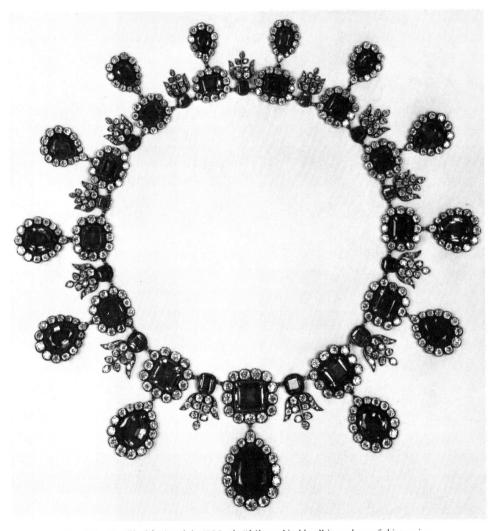

Bought by Van Cleef & Arpels in 1925, the "Liberty Necklace" is made up of thirty-nine faceted emeralds, either pear-shaped or square, surrounded by antique brilliants, and was accompanied by a pair of pendant earrings, each one composed of two square faceted emeralds, two small square faceted emeralds and two important briolette emeralds edged with antique-cut diamonds.

The Empress Marie-Louise's tiara, acquired by Van Cleef & Arpels in 1953.

THE EMPRESS MARIE-LOUISE'S TIARA

Attributed to the jeweler Nitot, mounted on gold and silver, this tiara was composed of eight pear-shaped emeralds, three square emeralds, four oval emeralds surrounded by about forty emeralds of more modest size—all probably "old mine"—and five hundred diamonds. The total weight of the stones was 250 carats.

Given by Napoleon to the Empress Marie-Louise on the birth of the King of Rome, in 1811, this tiara remained in the family until a Scandinavian descendant of the Hapsburgs sold it to Van Cleef & Arpels in 1953.

On certain exceptional occasions, Van Cleef & Arpels entrust some of their historic pieces to celebrities; in this case, Mrs. Marjorie Merriweather Post had the privilege of wearing the tiara to a function given in aid of the Red Cross at Palm Beach.

At the request of several clients and collectors, Julien and Louis Arpels agreed to exhibit the tiara (insured for four hundred and fifty thousand dollars, at that time equivalent to one hundred and sixty million francs) in the window of their Fifth Avenue premises in New York; subsequently they gave way to the pressing requests of certain clients who wanted to buy the emeralds individually. The sale of these emeralds took place between May 1954 and June 1956. As for the diamond-studded mount, it was bought by Mrs. Merriweather Post who had the emeralds replaced by turquoises. She donated it, in 1966, to the Smithsonian Institution in Washington.

The Empress Marie-Louise's necklace, which matches the tiara, acquired by Van Cleef & Arpels in 1953.

THE EMPRESS JOSEPHINE'S TIARA

Bought by Van Cleef & Arpels from the wife of an English lord during the last war, this tiara is the very one which Napoleon himself placed on his wife's head on the day of his coronation.

It comprises eight hundred and eighty diamonds with a total weight of about 260 carats, forming a motif of five butterflies arranged in descending scale and linked with bouquets of flowers. It should be noted that this is a tiara and not a crown because the circle is not closed and the two extremities are connected by a wide brown silk ribbon.

Having disappeared after the repudiation of Josephine, this jewel reappeared in 1872 in London, offered for sale by the Empress Eugénie in order, it would seem, to alleviate the hardships of exile. It is presumed that the Empress Josephine bequeathed it to her daughter Hortense, Queen of Holland, and that the latter gave it to her son, the future Napoleon III, which would explain why it came into the Empress Eugénie's possession. Madame de Metternich, wife of the Austrian ambassador, enjoying the confidence and friendship of the Empress Eugénie, was entrusted with the latter's jewels when she was obliged to leave Paris in haste during the Franco-Prussian war.

In her *Memoirs*, Madame de Metternich recounts how she received all the Empress Eugénie's jewels without their cases, higgledy-piggledy, wrapped in scraps of paper. She hid them in her apartments, in a linen cupboard, and a few days later entrusted them to the Count of Montgelas who dispatched them to London in a diplomatic bag and requested the Bank of England to store them in a chest without informing them whether the contents were the property of the Empress or of the State. Shortly afterwards, the Empress spent some time in London (where the Emperor died). The tiara was one item in the list of jewels that were sold by the Empress in May 1872. This tiara is in the collection of the New York branch of Van Cleef & Arpels.

*The Empress Josephine's tiara, which even now forms part of Van Cleef & Arpels'
collection, was bought from the wife of an English lord during the last war. It is made up
of eight hundred and eighty diamonds with a total weight of approximately 260 carats,
forming a pattern of five butterflies in descending size, linked by bunches of flowers.*

The Evolution of a Style

Elegance, spareness and proportion have always determined the aesthetic choices of Van Cleef & Arpels. The firm's ambition over the years has been to constantly renew the inspiration which initiates the creation of models without subjugation to contemporary taste, considered by the firm to be too ephemeral. While subscribing to certain rules of classicism, they have nevertheless been able to retain sufficient flexibility so as not to bridle the inventiveness and originality of the designer-creators. A humorous cover for an issue of *Rire*, which appeared in 1916, bears witness to the fact that, in addition to their consummate skill in displaying incomparable gemstones to their best advantage, they were also able to break with convention: a woman, clinging to the arm of her soldier companion, dreams in front of Van Cleef & Arpels' shop window; having set her heart on a piece of jewelry in gold and wood, she says to him: "Give me a piece of jewelry in wood, it will bring you good luck."

A piece of jewelry can be the result of one of two distinct intentions: on the one hand, to find the ideal design which will make the most of one or more exceptional stones, on the other, to find the stones that will fit into a precise design, a particularly attractive form; at present, very fine precious stones being rare, the first possibility is the most likely. A piece of jewelry arises from a number of designs which are reworked as often as is necessary, so as to translate on to paper the designer's creative idea. The project is sometimes transformed as it is refined; modifications are often based on simplification and restraint. Once the design is completed, it is translated into three-dimensional form, a scale maquette in sculpted wax is made and painted in gouache to represent each stone precisely, and this is then varnished. Sometimes replicas of the stones (*similis*) are placed in the wax so that the future piece can be appreciated to the full. In the case of certain pieces, rings or bangles for example, maquettes in boxwood—more rarely in metal—are made so that the shape can be refined without fear of error or waste. When the necessary adjustments have been made, specifications for executing the

Drawing of a pendant on an Egyptian theme made in the twenties.

Ill. p. 167, 168, 169

Drawing of a brooch-buckle on an Egyptian theme.

piece are established and the craftsmen move on to the actual making of the model in the specified precious materials. The final operation involves taking a wax impression of the finished article; plaster is poured into the mould and the cast thus obtained is carefully retained as a reference.

Van Cleef & Arpels' primary concern has been to create *parures* rather than isolated pieces and, accordingly, the same model is produced in all imaginable combinations of precious stones, semi-precious stones and even hard stones.

We shall attempt here, by describing certain significant models, to extract the principal tendancies which, over the years, have contributed to the personal and original style of Van Cleef & Arpels.

Archive records relating to jewelry made between 1906 and 1920 having unfortunately been lost; we shall begin our survey at the beginning of the twenties. At this time, the fascination exercised by the East over the Western world was augmented by the great archeological discoveries and travelers' tales. In 1922, the opening up of Tutankhamun's tomb by Howard Carter and Lord Carnarvon provided Van Cleef & Arpels with an inexhaustible source of inspiration. They celebrated this fabulous historical revelation in their own way by creating a number of pieces at this time—ribbon-bracelets, brooches, châtelaine-watches and vanity cases—embellished with pharaonic symbols such as the god Horus, the lotus flower, the scarab, the ibis and the sphinx, as well as certain hieroglyphs chosen for their graphic beauty. The jeweler's palette was enriched by the use of unusual combinations: cornelian and lapis lazuli; cornelian and turquoise; turquoise lapis and gold, and so forth.

Among the unique models created during the twenties, one of the first bracelets (made in 1923) on an Egyptian theme represented a frieze of scarabs and ibis in brilliants, rubies, sapphires and onyx; a brooch in the form of a rectangular buckle was decorated with pharaohs, scarabs and chained slaves, the whole being set with diamonds and *calibré* colored stones (rubies, emeralds, sapphires and onyx); a pendant, eight centimeters in length, suspended from a *chain-sautoir*

Drawing of a bracelet on a Chinese theme.

decorated with lotus flower medallions bordered with onyx, represented an Egyptian in profile bearing a tray laden with flowers and
birds.

Van Cleef & Arpels also directed their attention to China and
Japan; they incorporated, for example, the use, particular to Asia, of
jade, coral, pearls and enamel, the transposition of naturalistic decorative elements (a pagoda in the shade of a flowering tree, a dragon,
fishermen on junks etc.) or Chinese ideograms freely interpreted and
thus once again renewed the range of the House's creations. In 1924,
for example, on a flexible bracelet, they alternated vases of apple
blossom and Chinese characters in rubies, sapphires, brilliants, emeralds and onyx. A plaque-shaped pendant represented a pagoda in a
mountainous landscape. Not long afterwards they created a pendant
depicting a Chinese lantern in brilliants, rubies and sapphires,
which was worn at the end of a long *sautoir*. There was also a pendant in the form of a vase of flowers in the Chinese manner, which
was warmly received.

As for the Persian civilization, the delicacy of its arabesques and
floral motifs also nourished the imagination of Van Cleef & Arpels'
designers. Decorative motifs from carpets and miniatures were
transposed on to gorgeous bracelets; mosaics inspired them to create
veritable jeweled embroideries, notably on vanity cases. The subtlety of coloring—pink, jonquil, green, cerise, mauve—produced a
whole range of unexpected combinations: emerald and sapphire,
lapis and jade, and so forth.

This rediscovery of the East also influenced the tendency to use
stones which had been unjustly overlooked (topaz, amethyst, aquamarine, cornelian, etc.) and to oppose transparent, cut stones,

*Drawing of a pendant on an
oriental theme, depicting a
lantern.*

Ill. p. 282

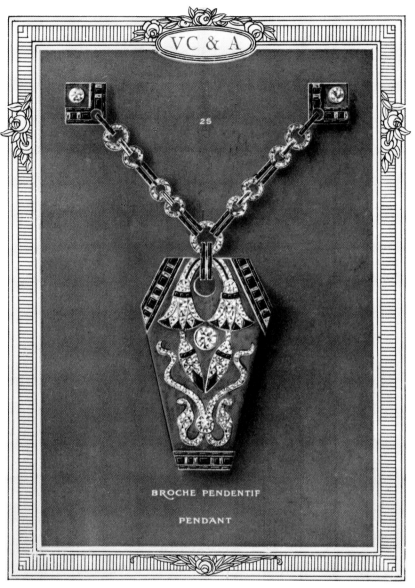

Brooch pendant on an Egyptian theme, from a catalogue of the twenties.

which reflected light, and matt, opaque stones, resulting in attractive and unexpected contrasts (emerald and turquoise, onyx and diamond, rock crystal and red coral, for example).

With happy results, the creators overturned the hierarchy of stones and boldly assembled, on the same piece, precious stones, semi-precious ones and hard stones; these models were termed "costume jewelry." We might mention, as an example, two brooches, mounted on gold, in the geometric style; one was composed of lapis lazuli, grey agate, coral beads and a ruby cabochon, the other of coral beads, grey agate, onyx and rock crystal. Superb necklets displayed similar combinations against a background of gold and black enamel in the geometric style: one, mounted on pale blue leather, combined loops and bars in lapis lazuli, and crystal and turquoise cabochons; another, on violet leather, combined grey agate, onyx and amber; a third, mounted on green leather, assembled grey agate, lapis lazuli and coral cabochons.

Drawing of bracelet showing the influence of India on jewelry designer-creators in the twenties. This was made of brilliants, emeralds, sapphires and rubies, 1924.

One of Van Cleef & Arpels' most characteristic pieces of jewelry in the twenties was undoubtedly the *sautoir*, which ideally complemented the tunic dress belted at the hip. There were infinite variations on this theme and the different combinations of colors and materials were fully exploited. As for the *chaînes d'huissiers* (Bailiffs' chains) in diamonds on platinum, they had the luxury appropriate to evening dress. The fashion for bare arms brought bracelets into *Ill. p. 148–151* vogue; up until the middle of the thirties, Van Cleef & Arpels created wide bracelets in platinum, flat and flexible, set with diamonds or sometimes colored gemstones.

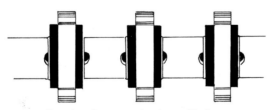

Drawing of a costume jewelry necklet in onyx, semi-precious and hard stones, circa 1925.

Page of bracelets from a catalogue of 1923–1924.

Facing page: Wide flexible bracelet comprising five sumptuous brilliants with a total weight of 27.01 carats, surrounded by interlacing motifs in brilliants, 1926. Enlargement.

Advertisement from the twenties.

Geometric compositions based on interlaced circles, rhomboids and squares incorporated stones cut in a variety of ways: baguette, trapezoidal, barrel, square and round. Sometimes outlined in onyx or black enamel, they formed the basis for a series of wide, flexible bracelets which were so light that elegant women might wear four or five at once.

Other models achieved great success: for example, a flexible flat bracelet composed of links of brilliants, connected by lines of sapphires, baguette emeralds or onyx and a narrow bangle in brilliants and onyx or in ebonite encrusted with a row of brilliants, emeralds or rose-cut diamonds.

At this time it was not unusual for certain women, confronted by the velvet tray on which ten or so bracelets set with precious stones were displayed, to be unable to resist the temptation to possess the same model in rubies, in diamonds, in emeralds and in sapphires.

Van Cleef & Arpels possessed the happy knack of being able to complement the fashion for short hair, cut *à la garçonne*, with long pendant earrings with motifs in the form of a drop, a pear, a cascade, *Ill. p. 158, 162, 166* or a bunch of fruit. They varied the play of colors and materials to infinity, using engraved stones, diamonds with jade and onyx, diamonds and lapis, diamonds with coral and onyx, or diamonds and onyx. Another model destined for success (and which is still worn today) was the "creole" earring, executed in a range of shades and forms.

The jewelry presented by Van Cleef & Arpels at the *Exposition Internationale des Arts Décoratifs* in 1925 celebrated the theme of flowers, a theme to which the House has always been faithful, despite the caprices of fashion: half-open roses—which were awarded a *Grand Prix*—roses in diamonds and rubies with emerald leaves, alternating on a wide, flexible bracelet with a matching brooch, or a garland of flowers on a ribbon bracelet in diamonds.

The House creators found unlimited scope for imagination and ingenuity in the multiple-use brooch: it could be attached to the

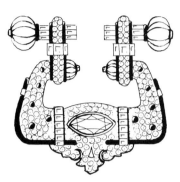

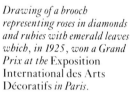

Drawing of a brooch representing roses in diamonds and rubies with emerald leaves which, in 1925, won a Grand Prix at the Exposition International des Arts Décoratifs *in Paris.*

Drawing of a broche-marteau.

cloche hat, to the shoulder or even on to straps and belts. The designers created model-types from which multiple variations were devised: bouquets of flowers in vases with geometric motifs were made as early as 1920 and were still being made up until the early thirties—ring-brooches, circles or ellipses in diamonds and rubies, or in diamonds, onyx and crystal. Sometimes they were embellished with a bow in brilliants and emeralds, or perhaps with still more flowers: a sprig of lily-of-the-valley or a chrysanthemum. There was the *broche-marteau* (thus called because it suggested a door-knocker), the bayonet brooch (a long pin with a decorative motif at each extremity), and the arrow brooch in onyx and brilliants, sometimes spiked through the center of a ring-brooch. And there was the famous feather brooch in platinum and brilliants, executed in different sizes.

Ill. p. 154, 155, 178, 179

Ill. p. 156

In order to feminize smoking jackets which women in the forefront of fashion were daring enough to wear, Van Cleef & Arpels, in 1924, launched a series of brooches in the form of bowties in diamonds, onyx and sapphires, or emeralds, diamonds and onyx; in the

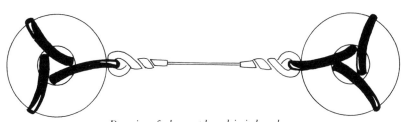

Drawing of a bayonet brooch in jade and onyx.

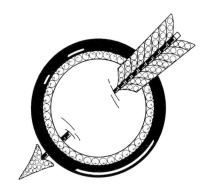

Drawing of a brooch in onyx and brilliants in the form of an arrow piercing a ring.

same spirit, they devised neckties studded with precious stones, and plaques, generally rectangular, completely paved with diamonds cut in various ways.

Departing from the geometric forms which were in fashion at the time, Van Cleef & Arpels' workshops produced an entire collection of jeweled birds: goldfinches, swallows, parrots, wagtails, budgerigars, and seagulls with shimmering wings which, in the form of clips or brooches, perched on the lapels of suits and even on cloche hats: they might even be used to fix majestic *aigrettes* in a whole range of colors! *Ill. p. 157*

Competing in popularity with bracelet watches, "châtelaine" watches and "*Régence*" watches met with great success. A minute watch face would be disguised by a cover set with precious stones which were often enhanced with onyx (geometric motifs, stylized vases of flowers and Chinese landscapes were among the decorative motifs used). *Ill. p. 302, 303, 307, 309*

Serti invisible (invisible setting), invented in 1935 by Van Cleef & Arpels, demanded long months of work by artist-craftsmen, highly skilled experts dubbed *grandes mains* or "master hands." A flower brooch might require as many as eight hundred perfectly matched rubies and in the resulting piece no trace of metal would be visible. A specially devised cut, giving each stone four additional facets, produced subtle effects of light and shade and the stones would reflect light as a mirror does. The secret of *serti invisible* is found in the underside of a piece: this is a net of gold into which each stone slots precisely. Assembled one by one, rubies or sapphires (emeralds were rarely used because of their fragility) slid into place thanks to special

Drawing of a watch-brooch in the form of a vase of flowers.

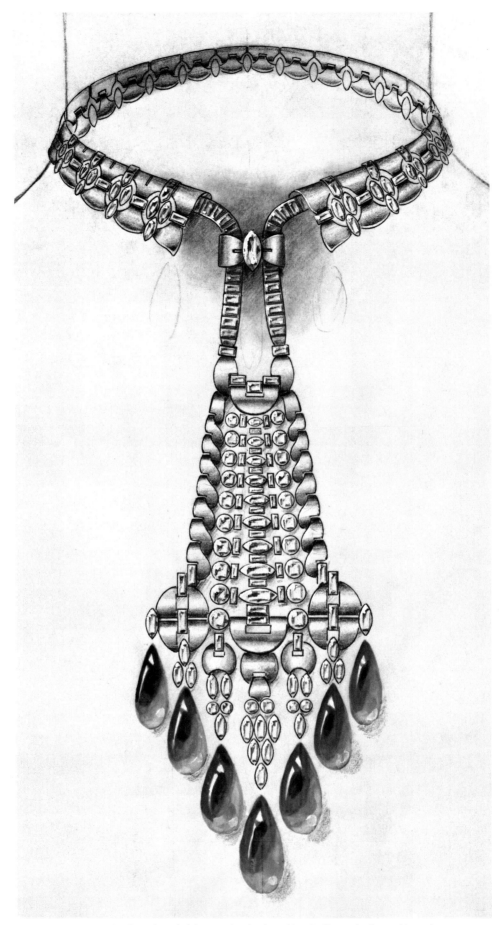

Drawing from the end of the twenties of a tie-necklace in diamonds, drop rubies and platinum.

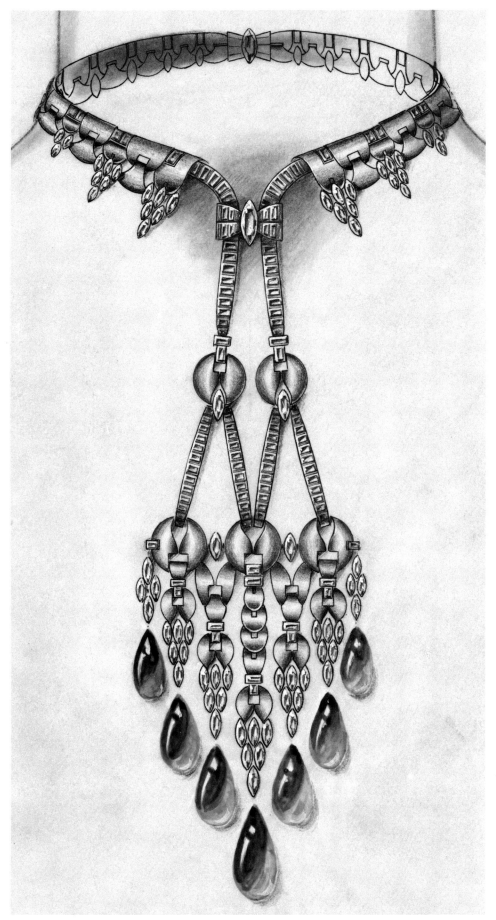

Drawing from the end of the twenties of a cravat necklace in diamonds, ruby drops and platinum.

grooves. Though they were usually square, stones could take on all sorts of shapes—triangles, trapeziums or irregular polygons—in order to fill spaces and marry with curves. When held up to the light, a piece of jewelry in *serti invisible* resembled nothing so much as a monochrome stained-glass window.

Serti invisible is a technique which allows the jeweler to model any form, any movement, and it has given rise to sumptuous pieces which it would be impossible to list comprehensively here. We shall simply mention the most remarkable pieces, currently sought after by collectors the world over: in 1935, the first *"Boule"* ring consisting of a swollen circle, convex on its upper surface, in Burmese rubies or sapphires; in 1936–37, an astonishing selection of unique brooches including the double ivy leaf or double feather (in rubies with diamond ribs); orchids in rubies and brilliants; the double holly leaf, fifteen centimeters in length, one in rubies, the other in brilliants (a variation of which was made for the Duchess of Windsor); a superb brooch depicting two peonies in rubies with leaves in brilliants and stems in baguette diamonds, which could be separated into two clips; a bushy, shaggy-headed chrysanthemum in Burmese sapphires, brilliants and baguette diamonds; and a rose with twenty-five petals in rubies, with emerald leaves.

During these same years, they also devised a wide bracelet in sapphires, of the *manchette* (cuff) type which was enlivened by a relief motif in baguette, round and emerald-cut diamonds and achieved celebrity through Marlene Dietrich. Another model had sapphire waves bordered with baguette diamonds suggesting a foamy crest. Certain cufflinks were also executed in *serti invisible*, as for example the *bâtonnet* model comprising two small sapphire cylinders, circled halfway up by a ring of brilliants. In 1948, in the ultimate refinement, a powder compact, lipstick case and mascara box were decorated in *serti invisible*.

Ill. p. 187, 189, 202–209, 234, 240, 255

The Duchess of Windsor wearing a necklace and earrings of faceted rubies and diamonds, and a large clip depicting a double holly leaf in serti invisible *rubies and diamonds, at the Bal des Petits Lits Blancs, Cannes, 1938. Photograph by R. Schall.*

Facing page: Drawing of the "Medici" necklace in baguette diamonds and brilliants, from which is hung a sumptuous faceted pear-shaped diamond weighing 30 carats, 1936. Actual size.

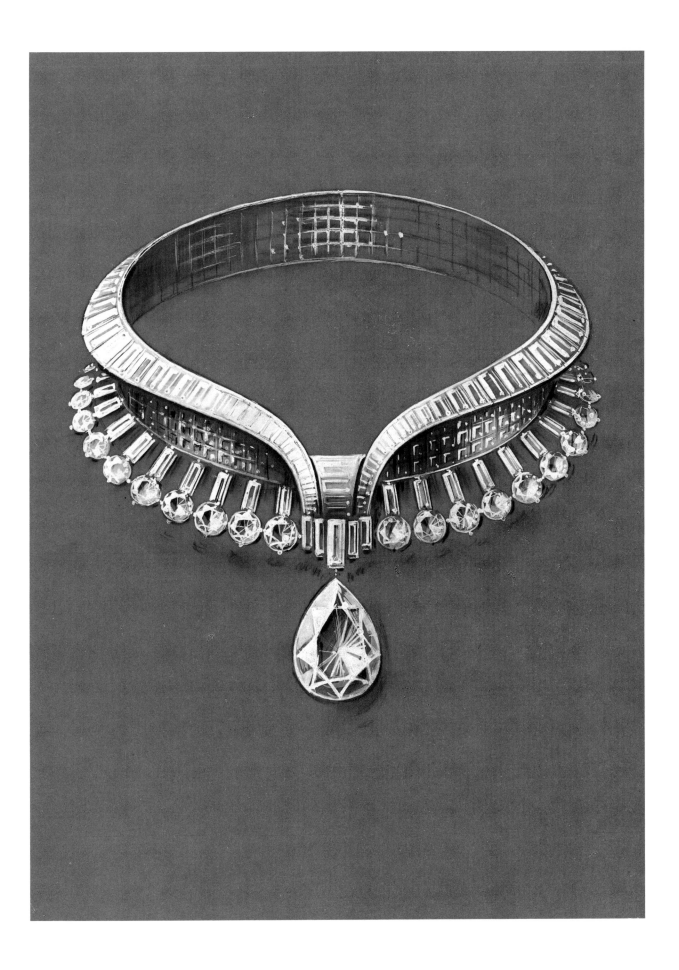

Advertisement devised by Pierre Simon in 1939 showing the model wearing a "Volute"
or "Copeau" *clip.*

Certain variations, imperceptible in models executed between 1930 and 1935, became more apparent from year to year and heralded the decline of the geometric style in favor of a revival of the figurative. Romanticism, grace and fantasy were among the new tendancies that were to come to the fore in the forties and fifties. Sharp angles, cut-off corners and flat surfaces disappeared and gave way to reliefs, curves, and volutes. Platinum was superseded by yellow gold which recovered its supremacy (though platinum was still favored in the realm of *haute joaillerie*). Important necklaces replaced *sautoirs*: some of these, inspired by maharajahs' necklaces, were composed of several strands of precious stones, others recalled coats of mail or fish scales. As early as 1934, brooches in the geometric style were giving way to the *Flamme* (flame) clip in brilliants and baguette diamonds, mounted on platinum. The latter could be attached, at whim, to an article of dress, to the hair, or to a hat (this model, a great favorite with the clients, was revived in the fifties). The following year, motifs nicknamed *volutes* or *copeaux* (wood shavings) in gold and colored gemstones, or—more luxurious—in brilliants and baguette diamonds on platinum, were once more to be found on brooches, detachable double-clips, necklaces and earrings. At the same time, a corsage ornament, somewhere between a necklace and a *fourragère*, met with great success. Composed of irregular volutes set with diamonds, it was attached to the shoulders and dropped down into a pendant on the left side. In the same spirit, clips in the form of cascades of ribbons in brilliants and baguette diamonds made their appearance, forming clasps on diamond necklaces or bracelets. They could also be worn separately. All these pieces of articulated, multi-purpose jewelry are absolutely characteristic of the Van Cleef & Arpels style. Necklaces could become bracelets, clips or pendants, thanks to secret hinges and invisible articulations.

One of the most famous of the House's models was created in 1934: the "Ludo" bracelet, a veritable ribbon composed of fine rows of rectangular polished gold plates, adjacent rows being arranged like bricks in a wall, which was finished off with a rich ornamental

"Bâtonnet" cuff links in serti invisible *rubies and brilliants, made in the thirties.*

Drawing of the "Boule" ring, created in 1935, comprising a gold ring, enlarged on its upper side, with serti invisible *Burmese rubies or sapphires.*

Capucine wearing a hat by Berthet with "Flame" clips created in 1934 and revived in the fifties.

117

Ill. p. 180, 187, 189, 205

Drawing of the "Double boule" ring, created in 1961, made in brilliants, serti invisible rubies or sapphires and platinum.

motif set with brilliants, baguette diamonds or cabochon rubies. Its creators devised other versions of which one of the best known is the model with the ribbon composed of a mosaic of small articulated hexagons in polished gold, called the *à ruche* (beehive) pattern, at the center of which—in the most luxurious models—a precious stone in *serti étoilé* (star setting) was encrusted. The clasp had a three-dimensional motif, termed *à pont*, a half-cylinder enclosing one or two short gold batons and sometimes batons in *calibré* rubies or sapphires set in *serti invisible*. The *à pont* motifs and the *hexagone serti étoilé* were produced for a number of years on rings, clips, earring motifs and bracelet watches. In contrast to the latter, yet other gold bracelets, in their volume and shape, recalled gears or ball-bearings.

Crystal, very fashionable throughout the twenties, was used in certain pieces of jewelry where gold links were combined with semi-circles or triangles of rock crystal joined together with gold pin-heads, or in signet-rings consisting of a convex crystal semi-circle mounted on gold or in clips of smoked crystal and brilliants. The models of the thirties followed the fashion for bracelets in emerald-cut diamonds, arranged in descending scale and linked by baguette diamonds mounted on platinum; the classic lines of these pieces raise them above the vagaries of fashion. The "four-leaved clover" clip, created in 1935, is one of the timeless models of the House (it was still being made in the sixties); it comprised four pear-shaped diamonds and four pear-shaped emeralds or rubies, with baguette dia-

Drawing of a bracelet composed of half-circles in gold and rock crystal, joined together by gold pins, circa 1935.

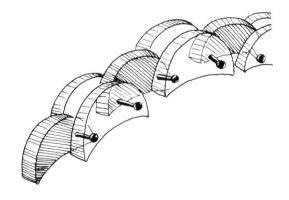

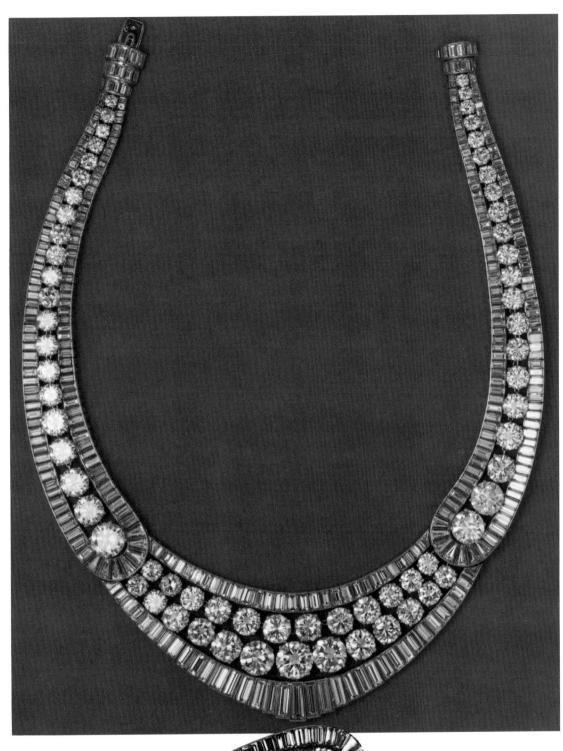

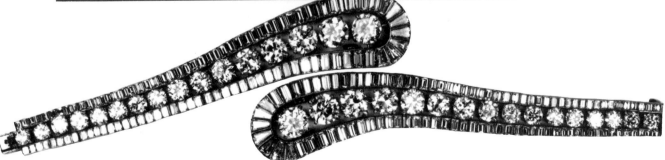

Collerette *of brilliants and baguette diamonds, which could be turned into a bracelet,*
1948. Actual size.

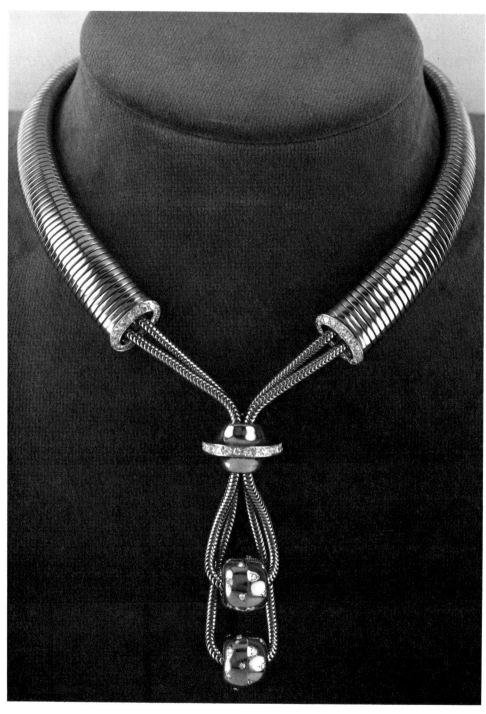

Necklace comprising a gold serpent chain and cord with gold bands set with serti étoilé *diamonds, 1946. Actual size.*

mond stems. From the original motif, rings and earring motifs were devised, as well as brooches with garlands or half-garlands of clover leaves within circles which might be open or closed. *Ill. p. 222*

Some of the pieces of jewelry which were very popular in the forties and fifties had made their appearance before the Second World War. Amongst these were the *Passe-Partout* clips, created in *Ill. p. 198, 226* 1938: notably the model with two or three flowers with corollas of cushion-cut Ceylon sapphires in yellow, pink and blue. It might be displayed on a suit lapel or be attached to a gold serpent-chain coiled round the neck, the waist or the wrist. This celebrated model was shown alongside other precious flower pieces: two marguerites with gold petals and a gem-encrusted center, or sumptuous models with interlaced leaves in gold set with diamonds, hung from a gold serpent-chain.

"Clover" ring of pear-shaped diamonds and brilliants, created in 1935.

One of Van Cleef & Arpels' most extraordinary pieces of jewelry dates from this period. Renée Puissant, Alfred Van Cleef's daughter, had a clasp devised at the Duchess of Windsor's request. Known familiarly as an *éclair* (zip fastener), in baguette diamonds on platinum, it was intended, of course, for evening dress. From this

"Four-leaved clover" clip in pear-shaped diamonds, baguette diamonds and a brilliant, mounted in platinum, 1952.

came the germ of an idea—developed much later, in 1951—of creating a "zip" jewel in gold, rubies and emeralds, the tag being adorned
Ill. p. 235 with a tassel of gold threads or baguette diamonds on platinum. It
could be worn open around the neck or closed as a bracelet and it became all the rage in the fifties. Another creation dating from 1938
was to win the favor of clients right up until the sixties: the "Hawaii"
model, a spray of tiny multi-colored flowers which, in their design,
resembled forget-me-nots. Assembled in bouquets on brooches,
they also appeared without stems on rings, ear-clips, bracelets and
necklaces. After the War, they appeared in the display-cases along-
Ill. p. 194 side another of the House's typical series, the swallow-brooches—
the swallow representing the return of spring—of which some
models, in the symbolic colors of blue, white and red, appeared in
groups of two or more, in a nest of plaited gold, on a straw hat or
even on a flowering branch. The following year, the bow motif reappeared, initially in a very flexible model composed of gold lattice-
work encrusted with diamond flowers with cabochon ruby centers.
Very different from models of the twenties, the bow once more
opened up an unlimited field to the imagination of the designers,
Ill. p. 218 who produced an infinite number of variations throughout the thirties, using different combinations of materials (precious stones,
white enamel, gold and platinum) and forms (rosettes, cockades, ja-
bots, single- or double-looped bows) on all types of jewelry.

The star of the forties, the ballerina clip (which appeared first in
Ill. p. 219 1945) with ballet shoes and tutu in polished gold set with precious
stones or studded with rose-cut diamonds, rubies, sapphires and
emeralds, was to become so famous that even now it is much sought
after at auctions by collectors. Other clips on the theme of the dance
were to complete this delightful range: Andalousians, *gitanes* (gyp-
sies) and *femmes libellules* (dragonfly-women).

From the thirties to the sixties, designs on the floral theme occupied more and more space in the designers' sketchbooks, provid-
ing them with an inexhaustible source of inspiration. Freely
interpreted, buttercups, asphodels, mimosa, daisies, marguerites,

"Ballerina" necklace of polished gold and brilliants, 1950.

Drawing of a bracelet of plaited gold leaves, made in the fifties.

Ill. p. 216, 217

pansies, hawthorn, convolvulus, anemones, lily-of-the-valley, violets, camellias, sunflowers, maidenhair fern and poppies flourished, singly or in bunches, on earrings, necklaces, clips and brooches, bracelets and rings. Though they were generally treated in a naturalistic style, some models, like the *rosace* (rose window) in gold with a center of brilliants, achieved such success that they were still in demand in the sixties. Another of the House's great classics, created in 1949, was a brooch (with matching earrings) composed of two flowers, one with petals set with jonquil-colored brilliants and a pistil of white brilliants and platinum, the other set with the same stones but with the colors reversed. The designers also excelled in multiple-leaf compositions which were mounted on either monochrome (diamonds and platinum) or multicolored clips, with ribbons of small leaves, plaited or twisted, arranged in chevrons or crossed.

Flowers were often combined with other themes: ribbon-lace in the "Valenciennes" bracelet, a frill adorned with marguerites, or, in the "Chantilly" bracelet, gold lace starred with flowers with diamond centers, or even the bow-theme, in rings of ruffled tulle crowned with "Hawaii" flowers, or with birds perched on flowering branches.

The whole range of technical innovations was cleverly exploited by the creators so that they could bend the precious metal to their will. Rings became turbans—wire-drawn gold, platinum and brilliants—they were *tressé* (plaited) or *quadrillé* (decorated with a grid pattern), there were flame rings in gold and rubies, or *tartelette* rings (created in 1948 and made until 1965), composed of vertical flutings and set with brilliants. Gold took on the most varied aspects: it was checkered, plaited, filleted, dotted, filed down, twisted, threaded, fluted, coiled, it imitated *cannetille* (twisted braid) or net.

Between 1940 and 1970, gold was required to reproduce the motifs or textures of certain fabrics—serge, herringbone, jersey, tulle or net—lace, trimmings—plaited or corded braid, tassels and pompoms—and even basketwork. A collection in *tissu serge* was launched in 1951: a clip composed of a ribbon with a single- or double-knot; a

"Tartlet" ring, created in 1948 and made up until 1965, composed of vertical flutings and set with brilliants.

"Double Palm" clip in osmior, platinum, brilliants, baguette diamonds and emeralds, 1957.

Drawing of a "Reverso" or "Double fan" clip which achieved great success in the fifties and sixties. This model was made in 1955 in gold, baguette diamonds, brilliants, faceted rubies, osmior and platinum.

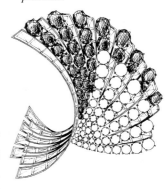

sumptuous flexible cuff-bracelet fastened by a buttonhole and button set with diamonds, or by a fluted emerald bead (one of these was acquired by Onassis); a flat necklace; a flexible *tissu serge* ribbon knotted at the side (a variation of 1953 consisted of a ribbon of plaited gold finished off with two arrows in brilliants) and another version close to the *tissu serge* cuff-bracelet, a gold ribbon fastened with a belt-buckle set with brilliants, the extremity forming a fringe.

Ill. p. 189, 234

In 1946, a double cord of plaited gold appeared, adorned with *pampilles* (pear-shaped pendants), wound round the neck and knotted at one side (one of these models was chosen by the Queen of Yugoslavia). The craftsmen's virtuosity is impressive, as those bracelets in the form of bow-ties with a flood of frills in gold tulle testify.

Ill. p. 220, 221

Sometimes fashion provided inspiration. The *col Claudine*, in particular, was transformed into previous metal which was worked in minuscule rhombs and fastened by two flowers in baguette diamonds and brilliants with jonquil diamond centers which could be detached from the necklace to embellish the lapels of a suit or the corners of a square neckline. Also created in 1946, a *pochette* (pouch) or *coin de mouchoir* (handkerchief point) clip was made in pierced yellow gold and platinum set with brilliants or rubies.

Yet other ornamental motifs enriched the individual style of Van Cleef & Arpels between 1940 and 1960. One of the most successful models, from 1950, was inspired by the cascade or falling rain for a clip (which could be attached to a baguette diamond necklace) and cascade pendant earrings (a single-fold knot composed of five or six long lines of baguette diamonds, terminating in *pampilles* composed of pear-shaped diamonds on platinum).

The lack of precious stones caused by the Second World War was succeeded by the return of sumptuous *collerettes* in the post-war years. One of these *collerettes*, created in 1951, was decorated with *rosaces* in cabochon rubies, faceted rubies and brilliants: the flower-motifs were detachable and could become earring motifs or clips. From this collection, the Maharanee of Baroda chose a sunflower *passe-partout* motif in gold and brilliants that could be worn attached to a necklace or on a serpent-chain around the wrist.

In 1945, snowflake motifs appeared on clips and they were to achieve a popularity comparable with that of the *capillaire* (maidenhair fern) clip. A series of bracelets and necklaces on marine themes portrayed waves in gold and brilliants or represented shells and fishscales. The *Tourbillon* (whirlwind) collection, launched in 1952, combined the shell motif with the helix: a double-shell for necklaces, a triple one for brooches and earrings. There was also a model in gold and diamonds for daywear and one in brilliants and baguette diamonds on platinum for evening wear.

The gold meteor motif, whose central core of platinum was set with diamonds, had a brilliant career throughout the fifties, during

Earrings suggesting a cascade or falling rain in baguette diamonds and brilliants mounted in platinum, 1953.

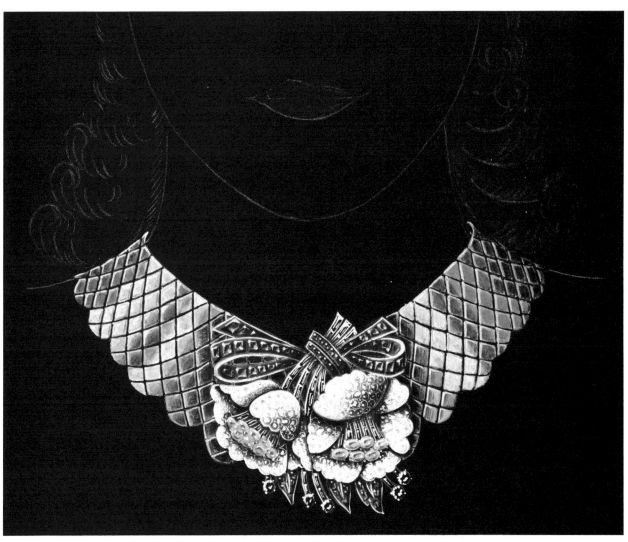

Drawing of a necklace inspired by the "col Claudine", worked in minuscules rhombs of yellow gold, with a clip composed of two flowers linked by a ribbon bow in calibré *emeralds. The petals are of white brilliants, the stems of baguette diamonds and the pistils are jonquil diamonds mounted in platinum, 1948.*

Model wearing a hat with "Snowflake" clips in gold and brilliants, created in 1946.

Drawing of a "Pochette" or pocket hankerchief
*clip in pierced yellow gold and platinum sprinkled
with small flowers of brilliants or rubies, created in
1949.*

which time designers devised a number of variations (the half-meteor or the off-center meteor) for rings, bracelets, clips and earrings. In the dishevelled style, very popular at the time, *coup de vent* (gust of wind) or *cheveux d'ange* (angel hair) necklaces and bracelets (1954) were made consisting of long rigid gold or platinum threads terminating in brilliants.

Other motifs, in gold or precious stones, adorned a range of completely original bracelets and necklaces: *fagots* (faggots), *jalousies* (blinds), *créneaux* (crenellations), *paillettes* (sequins); puzzle, fan, oat flake, rice grain, coffee bean, and pretzel designs; and the *forçat* (galley-slave), as in the bracelet dating from 1947, composed of gold links sprinkled with precious stones in *serti étoilé*. Other more luxurious models recalled plaits and twisted cords in gold and platinum, in a variety of colors, set with brilliants, sapphires, emeralds and rubies.

From 1948 and right up into the middle of the sixties, a bangle

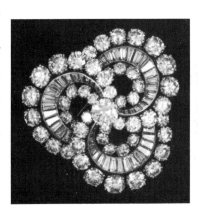

*"Whirlwind" clip, launched in
1952, in brilliants and
baguette diamonds mounted in
platinum.*

*Drawing of a bracelet inspired
by the "fagot" motif, fifties.*

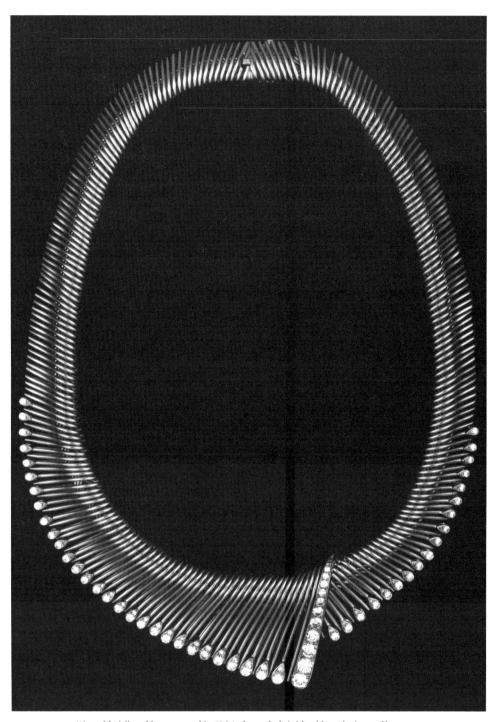

"Angel hair" necklace, created in 1954, formed of rigid gold or platinum filaments, tipped with brilliants.

composed of little gold beads was among the most famous of Van Cleef & Arpels' models. Several variations were devised and it was nicknamed *pelouse* (lawn), and took the name "bagatelle" when the gold beads were sprinkled with little "Hawaii" flowers. When it was decorated with bands or lines of brilliants and colored stones, arranged in diagonals, it took the generic name "Province," the different provinces being distinguished according to the combinations of stones: "Normandy" (sapphires, emeralds and brilliants), "Picardy" (rubies and brilliants), and "Savoy" (all brilliants). This motif was also found on rings, leaf clips and earrings. The same model was also executed in a version set with turquoise beads and sprinkled with little "Hawaii" flowers in brilliants and rubies, or sapphires.

Ill. p. 236, 246

The animal kingdom provided Van Cleef & Arpels with yet another source of inspiration: this theme was continually exploited and examples are so numerous that it is difficult to make a choice here. Above all we should note those sumptuous gold butterflies whose open wings displayed all the colors of the rainbow, the precious stones sometimes being set in *serti invisible*. Right up until the most recent collections, butterflies have gone through numerous metamorphoses.

An extraordinary collection of bird-brooches made its appear-

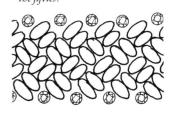

Drawing of a bracelet inspired by the rice grain motif, from the fifties.

Drawing of a "Camellia" earring, suggesting a spiral, in gold, platinum and brilliants, 1957.

This flexible necklace of gold and brilliants using sequin motifs was made in 1948.

Ill. p. 195

ance at the end of the forties. Fantastic multi-colored Birds of Paradise in gold and precious stones (sometimes engraved) were shown beside our more familiar birds, for example, the parakeet clip in gold, turquoises and sapphires, and the sparrow in gold, sapphires, turquoises and brilliants. It should be remembered that birds have always been a favorite theme of Van Cleef & Arpels, as for example in the famous ring of the fifties, nicknamed the "Lovebirds," sculpted in the form of two little birds in gold, platinum and brilliants with ruby eyes (the wings and tails are folded back to form the body of the ring).

Except for certain flowers such as the fuchsia, which in 1965 provided the inspiration for a clip and earrings with petals in rubies and sapphires (sometimes in *serti invisible*) and pistils consisting of a cascade of pear-shaped diamonds, naturalistic portrayal gradually lost ground in favor of stylization.

"Bird" brooch of brilliants set in gold, made in 1950.

The Arpels brothers' numerous visits to India prompted the creation of models directly inspired by the jewelry worn by maharajahs, but transcribed in the western mode. *Sautoirs* and *pampille* and cluster pendant earrings, abandoned since the thirties, were revived in the seventies, together with superb medallions which could be worn as clips or hung from *sautoirs*. In their design and color they suggested rigorously stylized flowers, rose-windows, the star motifs of Indian or Byzantine inspiration, or the Maltese Cross. As in the twenties, precious-, semi-precious and hard stones might be assembled on the same piece. In 1964 a gold necklace inspired by Hindu art combined brilliants and turquoise beads.

Jewelry was multicolored, with daring juxtapositions. The "Vallette" model (1972) was inspired by the impressive plastron *collerettes* which maharajahs wore over their tunics on official occasions: it combined gold, turquoises, amethysts, coral, green agate and brilliants. Still under the influence of India, the middle of the seventies saw the birth of a new fashion for beads of colored precious stones or *peau d'ange* (angel skin) coral, threaded onto a number of strands, either forming a plastron or twisted, embellished with jeweled cen-

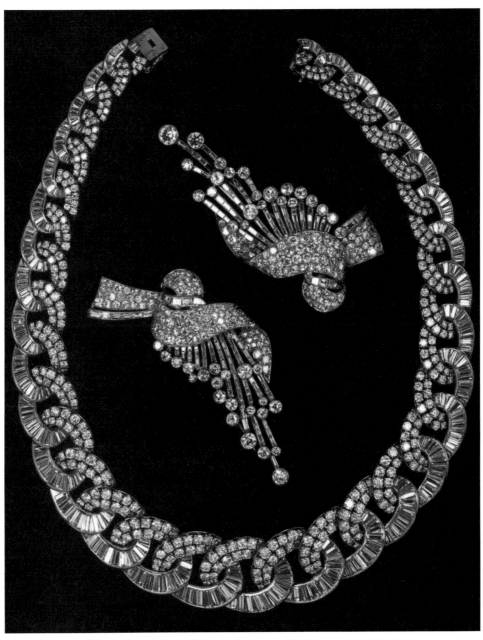

Necklace made up of rings of baguette diamonds and brilliants and a double clip in brilliants and baguette diamonds made in 1962 for Prince Ibrahim.

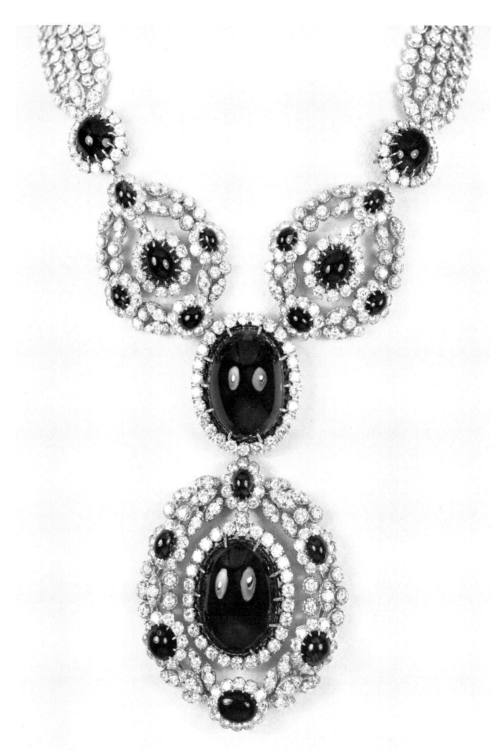

Made in 1972 for Her Majesty the Empress of Iran, Farah Pahlavi, this necklace of brilliants and cabochon sapphires mounted in gold can be separated to become a pair of pendant earrings composed of brilliants and twelve cabochon sapphires of 40.06 carats, a ring formed of a cabochon sapphire of 107.97 carats surrounded by brilliants, and a pendant clip bearing at the center a cabochon sapphire of 107.79 carats surrounded by brilliants and six cabochon sapphires. Actual size.

tral motifs (stylized flowers, lions' heads, etc.) from which hung tassels or *pampilles*. In 1974, a lion's head in gold and brilliants with emerald eyes formed the central motif of a long necklace composed of three strands of *peau d'ange* coral beads, holding in his mouth a *pampille* tassel of coral beads which were graded in color from light to dark. The following year, the lion's head motif finished off a twisted strand of white pearls.

The *sautoir-chain* is one of the most characteristic pieces of jewelry of the sixties and seventies: one of the House's most famous models, the *"Chevalerie" sautoir-chain*, created in 1968, was composed of gold links worked *en pépites* (to resemble nuggets, sometimes encrusted with brilliants) which could be separated into four elements and assembled in different combinations (long or short necklace or *sautoir*, belt, and bracelets). The *"Ségur"* chain was made in different materials, sometimes using links of gold or brilliants, or, in the Boutique version, onyx or wood.

In 1974, the *"Trévise" sautoir* and pendant alternated rhomboid motifs in brilliants festooned with gold with several rows of diamonds. The following year, the *"Barquerolles"* model was devised, composed of from five to ten strands of flexible chain worn either as a dog collar or as a *collerette*, embellished with *fausses navettes* (three brilliants circled with a twisted gold thread) attached to each other by motifs in brilliants of different sizes, and adorned with a *pampilles* pendant.

A collection of gorgeous *parures* were produced at intervals between 1975 and 1985: the "Gazelle" model, created in 1975 (a line of colored stones edged with two rows of brilliants, with a central medallion motif), was followed in 1976 by the "Lascaux" model, a rigid band set with brilliants and edged with polished *brut* gold with a lava motif; the *"Palmyre" parure* of 1979 owed its originality to the gap deliberately created between each brilliant and its circle of gold, something which added suppleness and intensified the brilliance of the stones. The *"Mélodie" parure* was thus nicknamed because it suggested a musical stave and consisted of three slightly spaced lines of brilliants on gold combined with short perpendicular lines of baguette diamonds from which pear-shaped diamonds were suspended (in another version, pear-shaped emerald cabochons hang from these lines). In 1981, the "Everest" necklace won all votes: a festooned and curled ribbon, with colored stones and lines of baguette diamonds alternating like precious tiles. A fabulous version of this model was executed in *serti invisible*. Three lines of brilliants mounted on gold, slightly spaced and arranged in a V from which pear-shaped diamonds were suspended, made up the "Lyre" *parure* of 1983.

Ribbons and bows inspired the designers to create new models such as the double ribbon earrings in gold and brilliants (1983); or the "Valia" *parure* (1985) where the rigid ribbon set with brilliants is edged with a row of baguette-shaped colored precious stones, embellished with a central bow motif. Inspired by an exhibition de-

Drawing of the "Everest" necklace, created in 1981, made up of a scalloped, undulating band, on which colored stones and lines of baguette diamonds alternate.

Drawing of the "Valia" necklace, created in 1985, the rigid band paved with brilliants and edged with a line of baguette colored precious stones and with a central bow motif.

voted to the history of lace, the Van Cleef & Arpels creators devised the superb "Valenciennes" *parure*: a *collerette* covered with a multitude of tiny flowers in brilliants mounted on gold, set in a delicate net composed of virtually invisible gold threads or *fils couteau*. They also turned their attention to draped motifs, in particular using as their inspiration the togas of antique sculpture; they transposed the folds into precious stones as in the *"Draperie Greque" parure*, composed of five rows of brilliants on gold. It is interesting to note to what degree platinum, for decades supreme in the realm of the *haute joaillerie*, was progressively ousted by gold from the sixties onwards. There are rare exceptions: for example, the incomparable "Ingres" *collerette*, created in 1971, with motifs of diamonds on platinum which could be detached and worn as clips, pendant earrings and bracelets.

The rich and eclectic imagination of the designers constantly obliged the jeweler-craftsmen to devise and perfect new techniques: they deployed prodigious powers of invention in order to be able to interpret and execute the dreams sketched out on paper. Pieces of jewelry, the objects of such fierce desire, can have as their origin a caprice of fashion or the development of a new technique.

"Ingres" collerette, *created in 1971, made in pear-shaped and navette diamonds and brilliants mounted in platinum. The central ornament can be detached and worn as a clip, and the two upper ornaments can be worn as ear drops. A necklet remains, part of which can be detached and worn as a bracelet. Actual size.*

"Valenciennes" collerette, created in 1985, strewn with small flowers in brilliants mounted in gold, linked together by a delicate net of invisible gold threads or fils couteaux. *Actual size.*

Top: Created in 1980, the "Melody" necklace, so called because it suggests a musical stave, is made up of three lines of brilliants spaced slightly apart, mounted in gold and joined by vertical lines of baguette diamonds suspending pear-shaped diamonds. Actual size.

Bottom: In 1983, Van Cleef & Arpels created the "Lyre" parure, made up of three separate lines of brilliants mounted in gold coming together in a V from which pear-shaped diamonds are suspended. Actual size.

This design was created by Gruau for a silk scarf made in 1981.

In 1954, the establishment of the Boutique department was tantamount to a revolution in the realm of jewelry. A project conceived by Jacques and Pierre Arpels, each year the Boutique presents a jewelry collection young in spirit and reasonably priced. The pieces are executed in very limited series and made with all the care employed in the *haute joaillerie* jewelry, alongside which they appear in the House's prestigious annual catalogue. The success of certain models has been such that they have remained available for several years so that the clients—for the most part French, in contrast to those of the *haute joaillerie*—have been able to acquire variations. When the Boutique opened, Van Cleef & Arpels revived the fashion for charms: these appeared in a new guise, either exclusively in gold or in gold and precious stones, and they were considerably larger than those previously worn by elegant women who wanted them in platinum. Throughout the fifties and sixties, the House renewed its models in

Drawing of a "Butterfly" pendant created in 1972: made in a range of sizes, in hard stones, lapis, agate, coral, edged with gold, it also existed in other versions, with wings in brilliants and body in hard stones or even in colored precious stones.

Made in gold with a tie in brilliants, this necklace is one of the "Or drape" (draped gold) series created in 1985. Actual size.

The X necklace, so called because the creators took this motif as their inspiration, was created in 1961 and made in gold and brilliants, or in gold, brilliants and rubies, or even in gold, brilliants and sapphires. Actual size.

gold, in gold and precious stones, and in semi-precious stones and hard stones each year. Anything might provide a pretext for the designers to create new charms. If it is impossible to give a comprehensive list of these, because there are so many, the following few motifs give an indication of the profusion and diversity of inspiration: thatched cottage, sailing ship, Eiffel tower, Vendôme column, desert island, birds perched on a branch, telephone, sunset, merry-go-round. Originating in 1958, the "Zodiac" charms are still great favorites. Equally popular are the animal charms which appeared on clips and became all the rage, some of the most popular of these still holding their places in the collections. The king of this fantastic bestiary is the "*Chat Malicieux*" from 1954, which was joined some years later by the "*Lion Ebouriffé*" (startled lion) (1962), and then the "Baby Lion" (1964). These presiding over a charming collection of good luck animals: squirrel, elephant, bear cub, owl, kingfisher, dachshund, hedgehog, rabbit, ram, fennec, sparrow, panther, tortoise, and so forth. The originality of the tortoise might be picked out for special mention: it is composed of half a walnut shell embellished with gold and brilliants and with emerald eyes. Sometimes the designers have translated the animal theme onto rings; for example,

The "Chat malicieux" clip created in 1954. The head is in gold, the eye an emerald cabochon edged with brilliants, the nose is a ruby, the body an onyx cabochon, with tail and paws in gold.

Drawing of a bracelet made up of alternate links of amourette *wood and gold, 1974.*

"Clematis" clip, which has matching earrings, in gold, amourette *wood and brilliants, 1972.*

"Philippine" ring, created in 1968, made up of a slender reed turned back on itself, encrusted with brilliants at its center and attached to a hard stone.

one of these, created in 1971, is composed of two ducks' heads in pink coral, emeralds and brilliants. One of the most celebrated models of the last fifteen years is the "Butterfly" pendant. Executed in different sizes in hard stones—lapis, agate, coral—edged with gold, it is also to be found in other versions with wings in brilliants and body in hard stones, or even in colored precious stones.

The designers have always remained faithful to their passion for flowers. Certain models have flourished in the Boutique catalogues since its inception: the "Pansy" clip; the "Convolvulus" clip; the "Kingfisher" *parure* (1958); the "Tobacco Flower" (1959); the "Laurel Leaf" (1959); the "Forget-me-not" (1960); the "Chrysanthemum" (1961); the "Cactus" and so on. Some years later, in 1971, the "Christmas Rose" clip and earrings in pink or white coral and brilliants achieved such popularity that it is still to be found in the Boutique windows alongside the "Alhambra" chains and earrings, created in 1973—gold chains punctuated by little four-leaved clover motifs in gold or hard stones, or even in mother-of-pearl—and the *"Petites fleurettes" parure*, dating from 1976, in brilliants and colored precious stones.

Since the mid-sixties, following the example set by the *haute joaillerie*, semi-precious or hard stones have been widely employed. In 1962, the "Twist" *parure* combined gold, a twisted strand of pearls and a strand of hard stones (lapis lazuli, coral, turquoises, green agate or aventurine). The "Philippine" ring, created in 1968, one of the Boutique's greatest successes, was composed of a slender reed curled back on itself, encrusted at the center with brilliants, and combined with a hard stone. The following year a range of earring motifs in gold and brilliants was devised, so that one could change the hard stone ring to harmonize with one's dress. In 1976, the interchangeable "Philippine" circles embellished a little pendant chain, so that the owner could have a different necklace every day. The "Lucrèce" ring, created in 1974, was composed of three rings in different materials: coral, brilliants and onyx. In some pieces, hard stones were ribbed, and their wide range of colors gave the designers the idea of juxtaposing them on the same piece of jewelry: accordingly, a gold pendant in the form of an anchor was enriched with coral, green agates, onyx, turquoises and brilliants. During this same period, other materials were rediscovered, and frequently combined with precious or hard stones.

"Twist" ring made in gold and pearls combined with a hard stone (coral, lapis or green agate), 1963.

An original idea, dating back to 1916, taken up again in the fifties and revived in the seventies, concerned the use of exotic wood (in particular *amourette* wood) combined with gold and precious stones: for example in the clip and earrings in the form of clematis flowers, or the curb-bracelet with alternating links of gold and wood. Ivory combined with gold for *sautoirs* (1973) or with horn for bracelets (1973), and mother-of-pearl on several pieces (such as the "Little Dog" in gold, onyx, brilliants and mother-of-pearl) were also often used. In 1981, the creators rediscovered grey mother-of-pearl; its iridescent surface was worked in small rectangles and combined perfectly with brilliants, pink coral or rubies on necklaces, bracelets or clips in the form of butterflies, clover leaves and florets. Hematite provided an equally attractive material: in 1980, in the form of little

"Mosaic" clip in gold, brilliants, coral, lapis lazuli and malachite, 1985.

145

beads threaded in several strands, it was made into necklaces with a central motif in brilliants in the Art Deco style. In other models it was plaited.

Van Cleef & Arpels played with the various shades of gold: the "3 Eights" ring and bracelet combined gold in three colors; the "Romy" *parure* (1978) was formed of fine alternating bands of yellow gold, pink gold and silver; the "Checkerboard" *parure* (1979) used little squares of white gold and yellow gold; the "Mikado" *parure* (1982) was a regular mosaic of white, yellow and pink gold; the celebrated "Philippine" rings with matching bracelets combined grey and yellow gold, the surface being sometimes fluted.

Some models from the Boutique collections became more precious at the end of the seventies. Favorite themes were plaits, draped gold, bows and lace: in 1983 *"cols Claudines"* in gold tulle, sprinkled with little flowers in brilliants, were revived and worn as *collerettes*; clips and earrings in the form of bows in gold tulle were followed by *"Nattes Tressées"* (plaits) in pearls, green agate beads or hematite. They were fastened by a central interchangeable motif in gold and brilliants. Two creations of 1985, the superb "draped gold" *parure* knotted with threads of brilliants and the "Mosaic" *parure*, consisting of a marquetry of hard stones and brilliants, give one an idea of the beauty of future creations of the Boutique.

"Ladybird" ring, made in gold, coral, brilliants and onyx, 1970.

Illustration by Jean Dupas for the cover of the 1925 catalogue.

*All the jewelry of Van Cleef & Arpels is signed and carries an identification number
accompanied by the logo reproduced here.*

Art Deco bracelet in navette, baguette and triangular diamonds, brilliants and calibré *emeralds, mounted in platinum, 1924.*

Flexible Art Deco bracelet in brilliants, baguette emeralds and onyx, mounted in platinum.

Art Deco bracelet in baguette and square diamonds, brilliants and emerald-cut sapphires mounted in platinum. Private collection.

Art Deco bracelet made up of five cabochon sapphires, baguette diamonds and brilliants mounted in platinum, circa 1926.

Facing page: Ribbon Art Deco bracelet in brilliants—the largest weighing 15.71 carats—mounted in platinum, 1924. Enlargement.

Page from the 1923 catalogue: an Art Deco bracelet of cabochon rubies and diamonds in platinum; an Art Deco bracelet of diamonds in platinum; a bracelet of emeralds and diamonds in platinum; an Art Deco bracelet of diamonds in platinum; a bracelet of baguette, square and triangular diamonds, brilliants and octagonal faceted rubies mounted in platinum. Enlargement.

Page from the 1923 catalogue: an Art Deco bracelet of baguette and square diamonds, brilliants and square emeralds in platinum; an Art Deco bracelet of calibré rubies and brilliants in platinum; an Art Deco bracelet made up of interlaced rings of faceted sapphires and brilliants in platinum; an Art Deco bracelet with five oval cabochon rubies and brilliants in platinum; an Art Deco bracelet of onyx cut to fit and brilliants in platinum. Enlargement.

Art Deco brooch of baguette, half-moon and trapezoidal diamonds and brilliants, in platinum, 1931. Van Cleef & Arpels collection. Enlargement.

Art Deco brooch comprising a ring and a flexible band of baguette diamonds and brilliants in platinum, 1931. Van Cleef & Arpels collection. Enlargement.

Facing page: Necklace of navette and baguette diamonds and brilliants in platinum, 1928. Van Cleef & Arpels collection. Enlargement.

152

Page from the 1923 catalogue: an Art Deco ring brooch of onyx and diamonds in platinum; an Art Deco ring brooch of crystal, onyx and diamonds in platinum; an Art Deco ring brooch of brilliants, baguette and square diamonds and onyx in platinum. Enlargement.

Page from the 1923 catalogue: an Art Deco "Interlace" clip of diamonds, calibré *rubies with a central cabochon ruby, in platinum; an Art Deco clip of onyx,* calibré *emeralds and diamonds in platinum; an Art Deco "Bow-tie" with flower motifs, in sapphires, onyx and diamonds in platinum. Enlargement.*

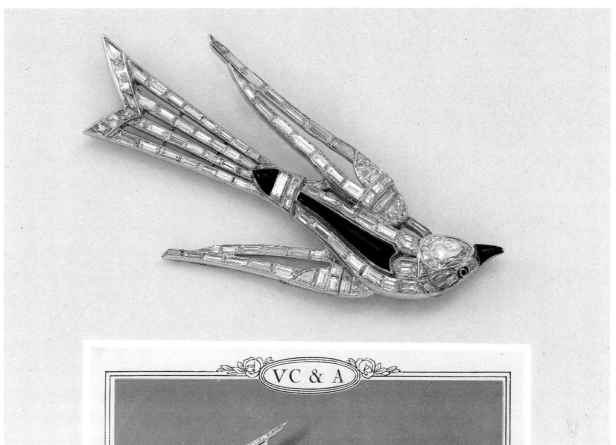

Above: "Swallow" clip of baguette diamonds and onyx with a pear-shaped diamond head, in platinum, 1928. Van Cleef & Arpels collection. Enlargement.

Left: "Bird" clip of diamonds mounted in platinum which could also be worn as a hat pin with feathers. 1922 Catalogue.

Facing page: "Feather" clip of brilliants in platinum, 1927. Van Cleef & Arpels collection. Enlargement.

Page from the 1923 catalogue: five Art Deco pendant earrings of baguette, navette, triangular, trapezoidal and square diamonds, brilliants, calibré emeralds and an emerald drop, mounted in platinum. Enlargement.

Facing page: Art Deco clip of brilliants, baguette and navette diamonds and five drop emeralds, in platinum, made in 1928 for Princess Hohenlohe. Van Cleef & Arpels collection. Enlargement.

Drawing of a collerette of emerald-cut, baguette, trapezoidal, half-moon and square diamonds and twelve drop emeralds in platinum, 1930. Reduction.

Art Deco pendant and chain with geometric motifs and fringe, of baguette diamonds and brilliants with a central octagonal faceted emerald, in platinum, from the 1925 catalogue. Enlargement.

Pendant earrings of baguette diamonds, brilliants and baguette sapphires in platinum, 1923. Van Cleef & Arpels collection. Enlargement.

Facing page: Bracelet with jeweled tassel, comprising five emerald-cut rubies (15.26 carats), baguette diamonds and brilliants in platinum, 1929. Van Cleef & Arpels collection. Enlargement.

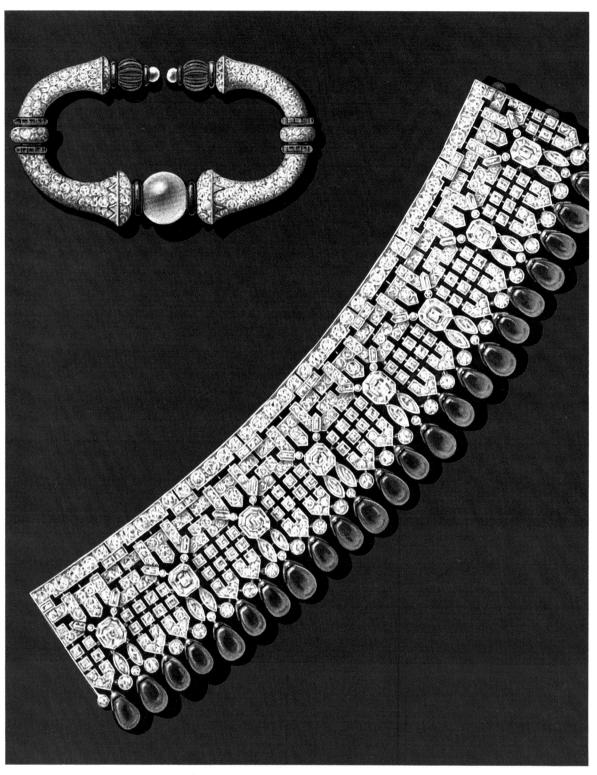

Bangle of engraved emeralds and calibré *emeralds, diamonds, three pearls and onyx, in platinum. Enlargement.*

Wide "cuff" bracelet in the Indian style, with geometric motifs in emerald-cut, baguette and navette diamonds, brilliants and twenty-three drop emeralds in platinum. These two bracelets are reproduced from the 1925 catalogue. Enlargement.

Art Deco bracelet of brilliants with three exceptional cabochon emeralds, in platinum,
reproduced from the 1925 catalogue. Enlargement.

Brooch or belt-buckle with Pharaonic Egyptian motifs, in rubies, calibré emeralds, onyx and diamonds, in platinum, circa 1924. Van Cleef & Arpels collection.

Facing page: Art Deco pendant earrings of diamonds, coral, onyx and pearls, in platinum, 1922. Private collection, New York; Art Deco bracelet of diamonds, coral and onyx, in platinum, 1923. Private collection, New York; Art Deco brooch of diamonds, ribbed onyx and engraved coral, in platinum, 1923. Private collection, New York. Enlargement.

Details of a flexible bracelet with motifs from Pharaonic Egypt made of diamonds,
sapphires, rubies and calibré *emeralds, mounted in platinum, circa 1924.*
Enlargement.

Facing page: Flexible bracelet with motifs from Pharaonic Egypt, in rubies, emeralds,
sapphires, onyx and diamonds, in platinum, 1924. Van Cleef & Arpels collection.
Enlargement.

Gouache designs for bracelets in platinum, faceted rubies, brilliants and baguette diamonds, projects carried out between 1926 and 1930.

Facing page: Bracelet with three emerald-cut rubies, seventy-two square rubies, half-moon and baguette diamonds and brilliants mounted in platinum.

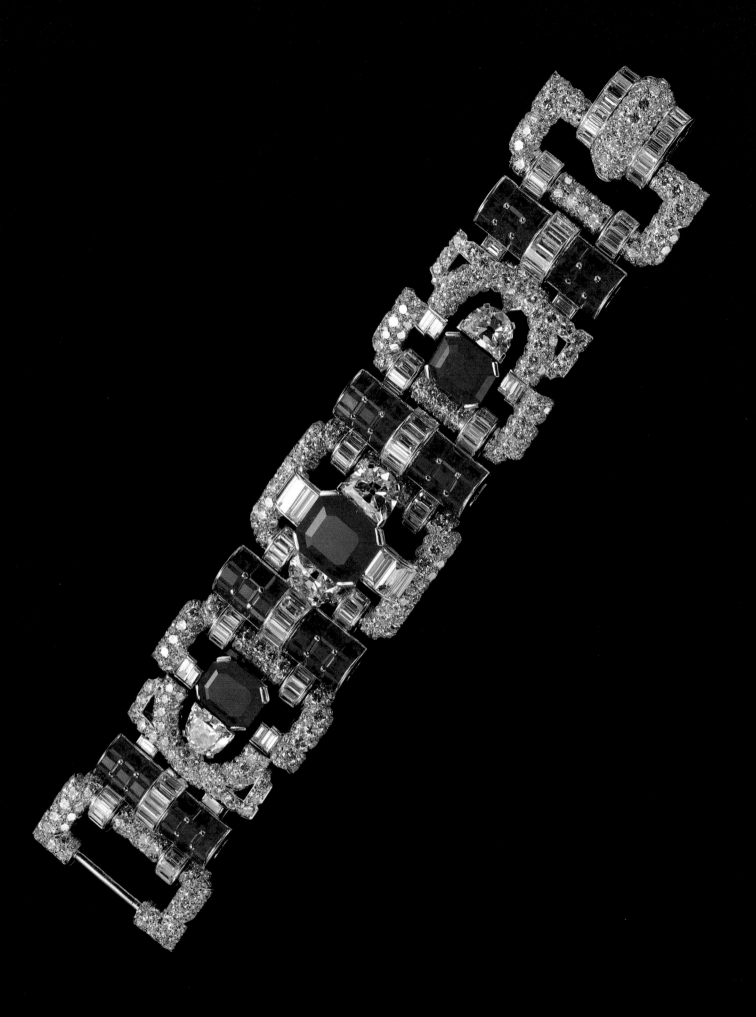

Gouache design for a necklace of cabochon sapphires, emerald-cut sapphires and baguette diamonds in platinum, circa 1932 (project carried out).

Gouache design for a necklace of ruby beads, baguette diamonds and brilliants in platinum, circa 1932 (project carried out).

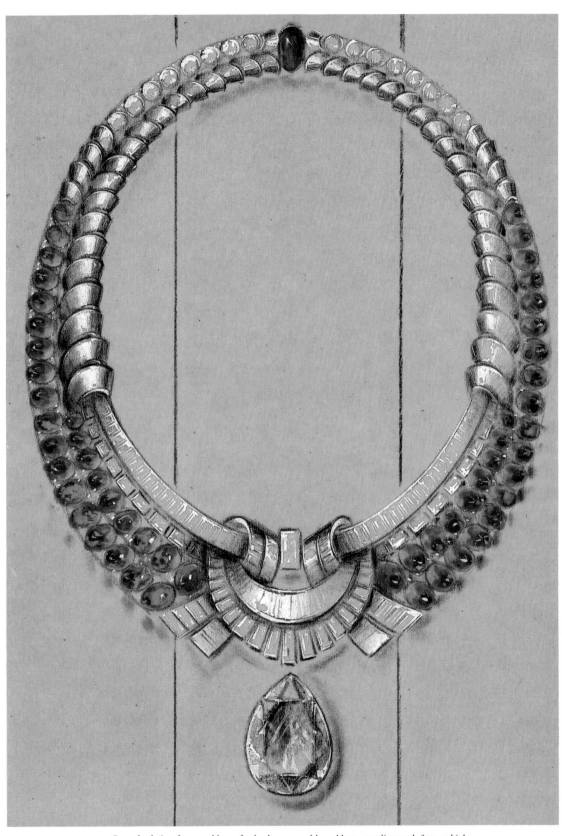

*Gouache design for a necklace of cabochon emeralds and baguette diamonds from which
an exceptional pear-shaped diamond of 55 carats is suspended, circa 1931.*

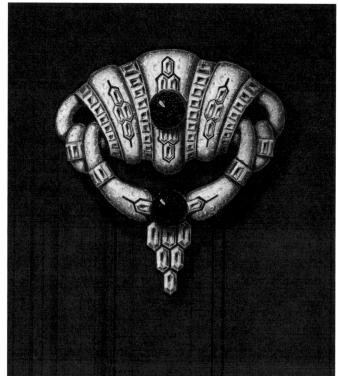

Gouache design for a brooch with an important emerald-cut emerald, baguette diamonds and brilliants in platinum, circa 1929.

Gouache design for a clip with two emerald cabochons, baguette diamonds and brilliants in platinum, circa 1929.

Facing page: Necklace of cabochon emeralds and baguette diamonds in platinum, 1938. Private collection. Enlargement.

A project by René-Sim Lacaze, intended for the catalogue at the end of 1939 with a preface by Paul Valéry (not published because of the declaration of war).

Facing page: Necklace of baguette diamonds and oval faceted rubies in platinum, 1937. Private collection. Enlargement.

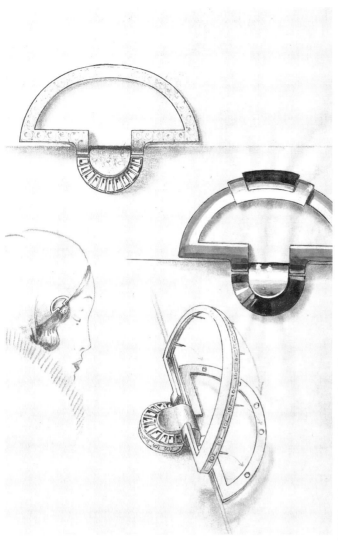

Clips for the hat, handbag or corsage, made of bands of diamonds in platinum or in polished or white gold with turquoise and lapis.

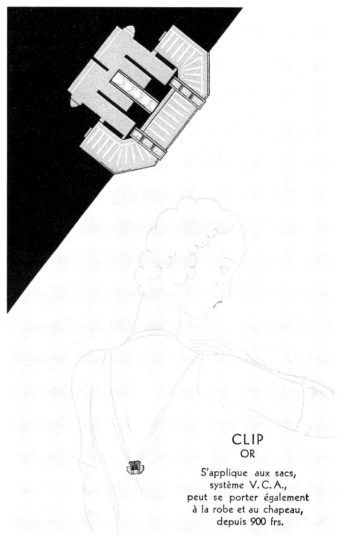

CLIP
OR

S'applique aux sacs,
système V.C.A.,
peut se porter également
à la robe et au chapeau,
depuis 900 frs.

Clip in gold and brilliants, circa 1930.

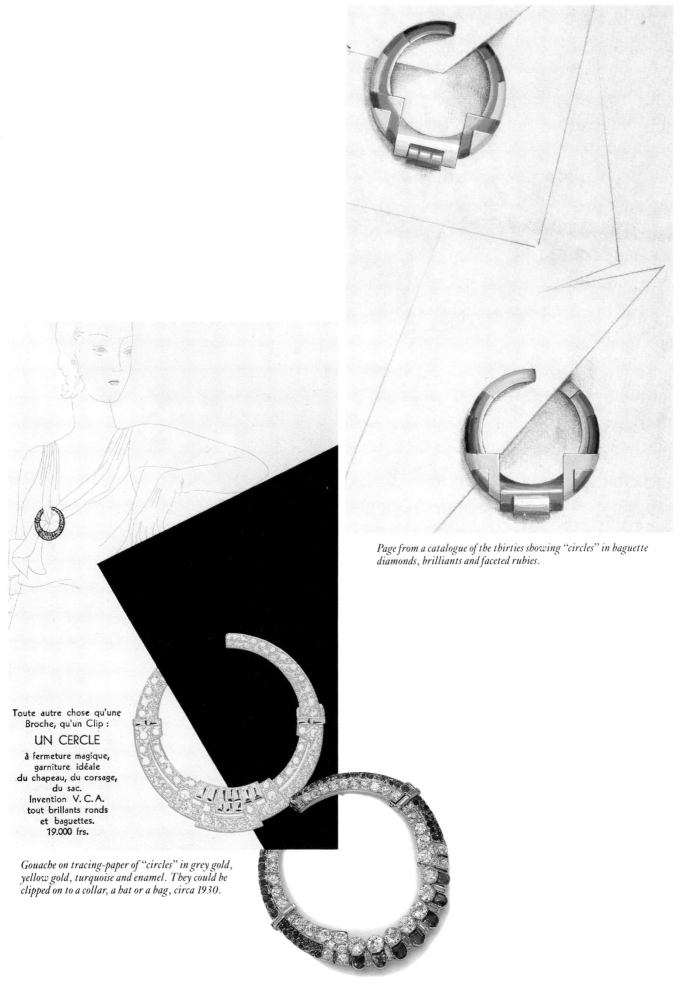

Page from a catalogue of the thirties showing "circles" in baguette diamonds, brilliants and faceted rubies.

Toute autre chose qu'une
Broche, qu'un Clip :
UN CERCLE
à fermeture magique,
garniture idéale
du chapeau, du corsage,
du sac.
Invention V.C.A.
tout brillants ronds
et baguettes.
19.000 frs.

Gouache on tracing-paper of "circles" in grey gold, yellow gold, turquoise and enamel. They could be clipped on to a collar, a hat or a bag, circa 1930.

179

Gouache design for a detail from a "Ludo-Hexagone" cuff-bracelet, made up of a mosaic of small polished gold hexagons, called à ruches *(beehive) and with detailing in baguette diamonds and brilliants on platinum, circa 1938.*

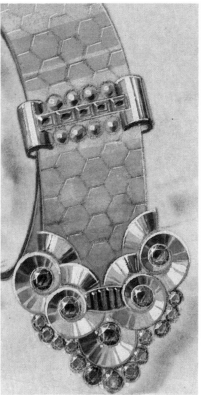

Gouache design for a detail from a "Ludo-Hexagone" cuff-bracelet made up of a mosaic of small polished gold hexagons, called à ruches *(beehive) and a motif in* calibré *and round faceted sapphires, circa 1938.*

Facing page: Bracelet in polished gold, round faceted and square emeralds on gold, brilliants on platinum, circa 1940. Private collection. Enlargement.

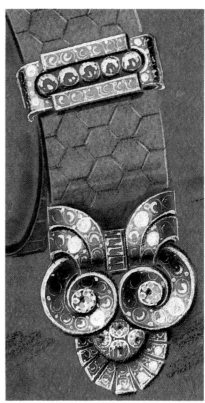

Gouache design for a detail from a "Ludo-Hexagone" cuff-bracelet, made up of a mosaic of small polished gold hexagons, called à ruches *(beehive) and with a decoration in baguette diamonds and brilliants on platinum, circa 1938.*

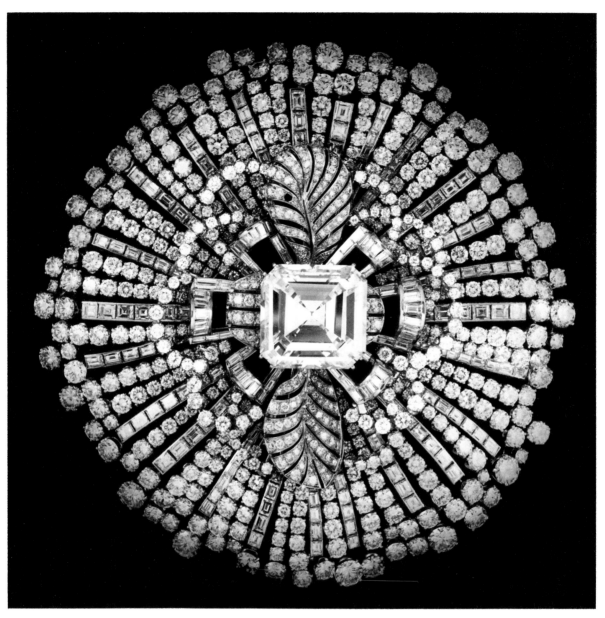

Corsage ornament altered during the forties, with an exceptional emerald-cut diamond, baguette diamonds and brilliants. Actual size.

Facing page: Bracelet made up of five emerald-cut diamonds alternating with square diamonds surrounded by baguette diamonds and brilliants, with a half-moon fastening, in platinum, 1935. Van Cleef & Arpels collection. Enlargement.

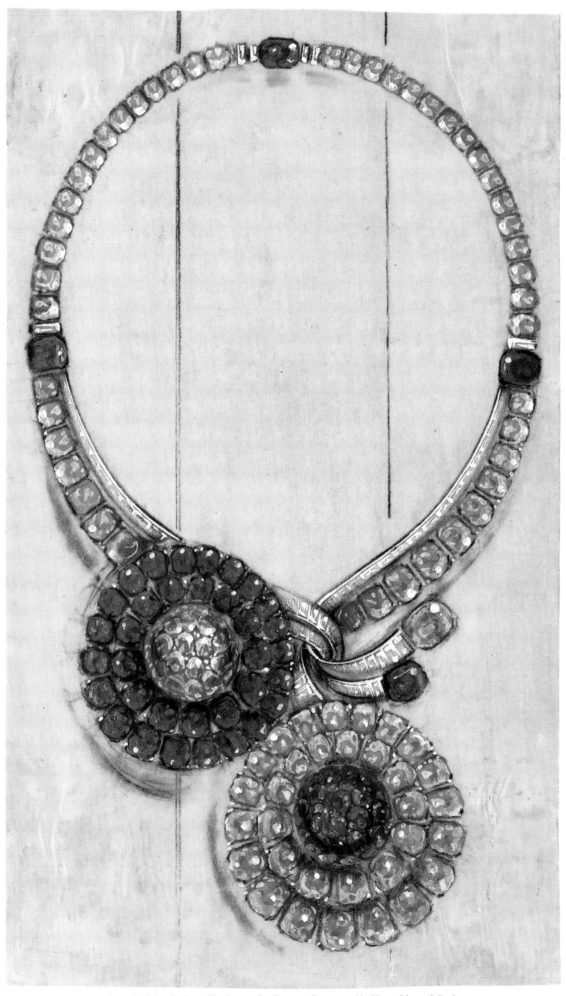

Gouache design by René-Sim Lacaze for Countess Camargo. Necklace of faceted Ceylon sapphires and Burmese sapphires and baguette diamonds, 1938. Enlargement. René-Sim Lacaze collection.

Facing page: Necklace of emerald-cut sapphires, oval faceted sapphires and baguette diamonds in platinum, 1936. Enlargement.

Necklace of polished gold and citrines, circa 1935.

Facing page: "Ludo-Hexagone" *bracelet made of a mosaic of little articulated hexagons in polished gold, called* à ruches *(beehive), with* serti étoilé *rubies. The clasp has a three-dimensional* "à pont" *motif in* serti invisible *rubies and a half-circle of brilliants. The bracelet has two matching clips, 1936. Lewis M. Kaplan, London.*

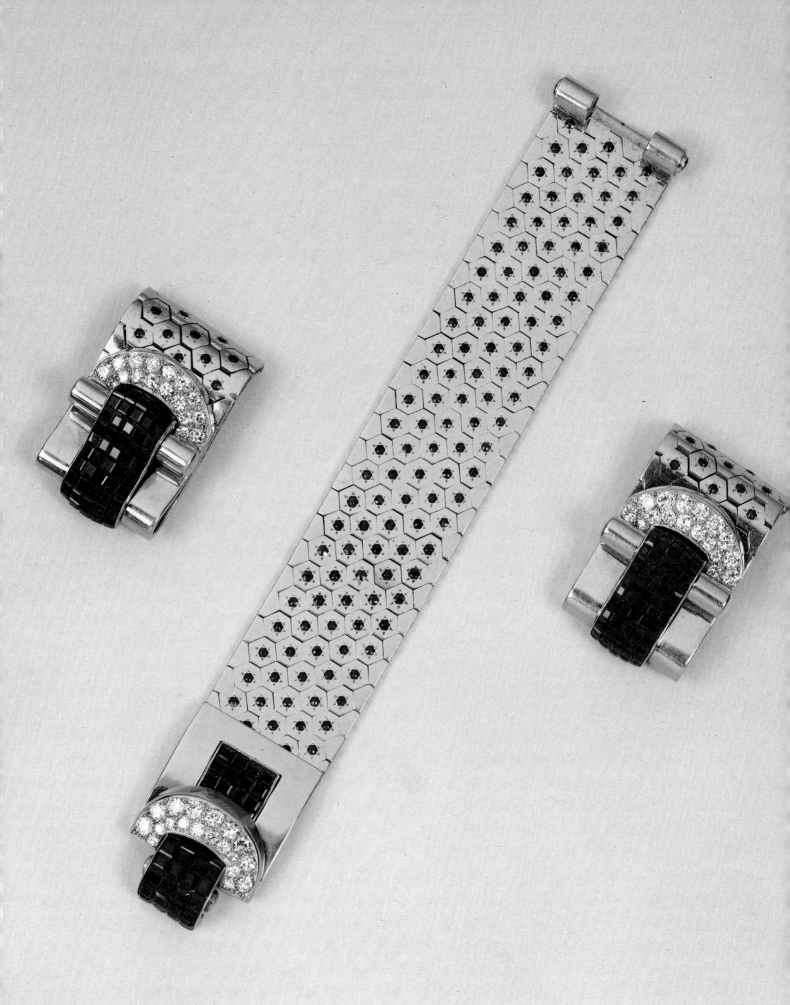

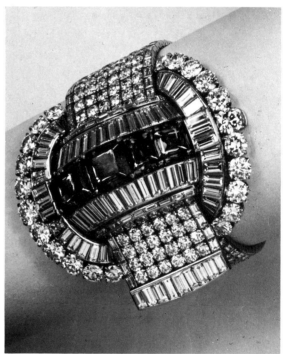

"Marguerite" clip of cabochon emeralds, brilliants and gold attached to a "serpent chain" bracelet, 1946. Enlargement.

Detachable "Volutes" double clip, could be attached to a special mount and worn as a bracelet. It was made of baguette diamonds mounted in platinum and gold, 1937. Enlargement.

"Rouleau" bracelet of baguette diamonds and brilliants in platinum, 1938. Enlargement.

Bracelet with four emerald-cut emeralds, baguette diamonds and brilliants in platinum, 1936. Enlargement.

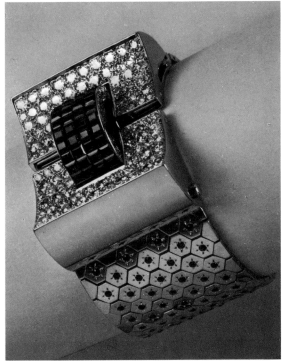

"Ludo-Hexagone" *bracelet made up of a mosaic of little articulated hexagons in polished gold,* à ruches *(beehive) with a* serti étoilé *ruby at each center. The clasp has a three-dimensional* à pont *motif in* serti invisible *rubies surrounded by a ground of brilliants, circa 1938. Enlargement.*

"Cuff" *bracelet of brilliants and oval faceted sapphires in platinum, 1962. Enlargement.*

"Cuff" *bracelet in cloth of gold with a clasp in the form of a bead-button in twisted gold wire and brilliants, passed through a button-hole, 1951. Enlargement.*

"Buckle" *bracelet in oval faceted sapphires and brilliants on platinum, 1968. Enlargement.*

*Gouache design by René-Sim Lacaze for a commission by Countess Camargo for a double
clip and earrings of faceted rubies and diamonds, 1937. René-Sim Lacaze collection.*

Flower clip in polished gold and brilliants, 1938.
Private collection. Enlargement.

"Posy" clip in polished gold with translucent blue
enamel petals and centers in brilliants, 1938. Van
Cleef & Arpels collection. Enlargement.

*Double clip of baguette
diamonds and brilliants
mounted in platinum,
separable into two clips, 1937.
Van Cleef & Arpels collection.*

*Double clip of baguette
diamonds and brilliants
mounted in platinum,
separable into two clips
(right), 1938. Van Cleef &
Arpels collection.*

"Flot de rubans" *clip of baguette diamonds and
brilliants in platinum, 1937. Van Cleef &
Arpels collection.*

Earrings of oval faceted sapphires, baguette diamonds and brilliants in platinum, 1935. Van Cleef & Arpels collection. Enlargement.

"Bow" brooch of baguette diamonds and brilliants in platinum, 1934. Enlargement.

Brooch of baguette diamonds, brilliants and emeralds, 1937. Private collection. Enlargement.

"Hat" clip in woven gold with two nesting swallows in brilliants with ruby eyes, surrounded by "Hawaii" flowers in faceted and calibré *rubies, faceted sapphires and brilliants, 1946. Van Cleef & Arpels collection. Enlargement.*

Clip with two flowers tied with a ribbon of jonquil diamonds in gold; the petals are of white brilliants, the center of jonquil diamonds, the stems of baguette diamonds, 1938. Van Cleef & Arpels collection.

Facing page: "Bird of Paradise" clip: the feathers are in calibré *sapphires and rubies on gold, the body in engraved and polished gold, the beak of brilliants in platinum and the eye is a ruby cabochon, 1942. Private collection. Enlargement.*

Gouache design for a pearl necklace with a flower clip of diamonds. The pearls which hang down have pendant tassels of diamonds, circa 1950.

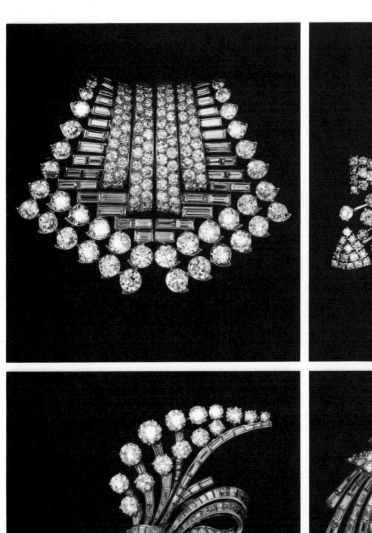

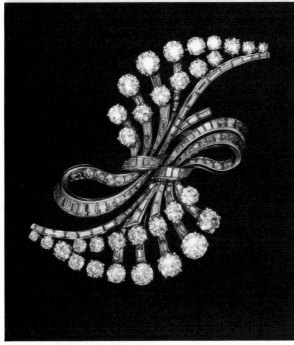

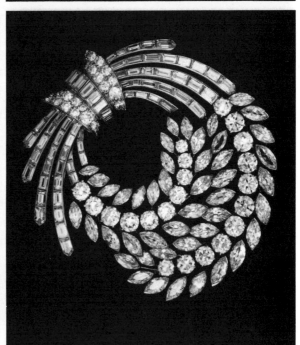

Double clip of baguette diamonds and brilliants in platinum, separable into two clips which could be worn on either side of a square neckline, 1939.

Double clip of baguette diamonds and brilliants in platinum, separable into two clips, 1951.

"Capillaire" (maidenhair fern) clip in polished gold and brilliants, 1946.

"Gerbe" (sheaf) clip of baguette and navette diamonds and brilliants in platinum, 1939.

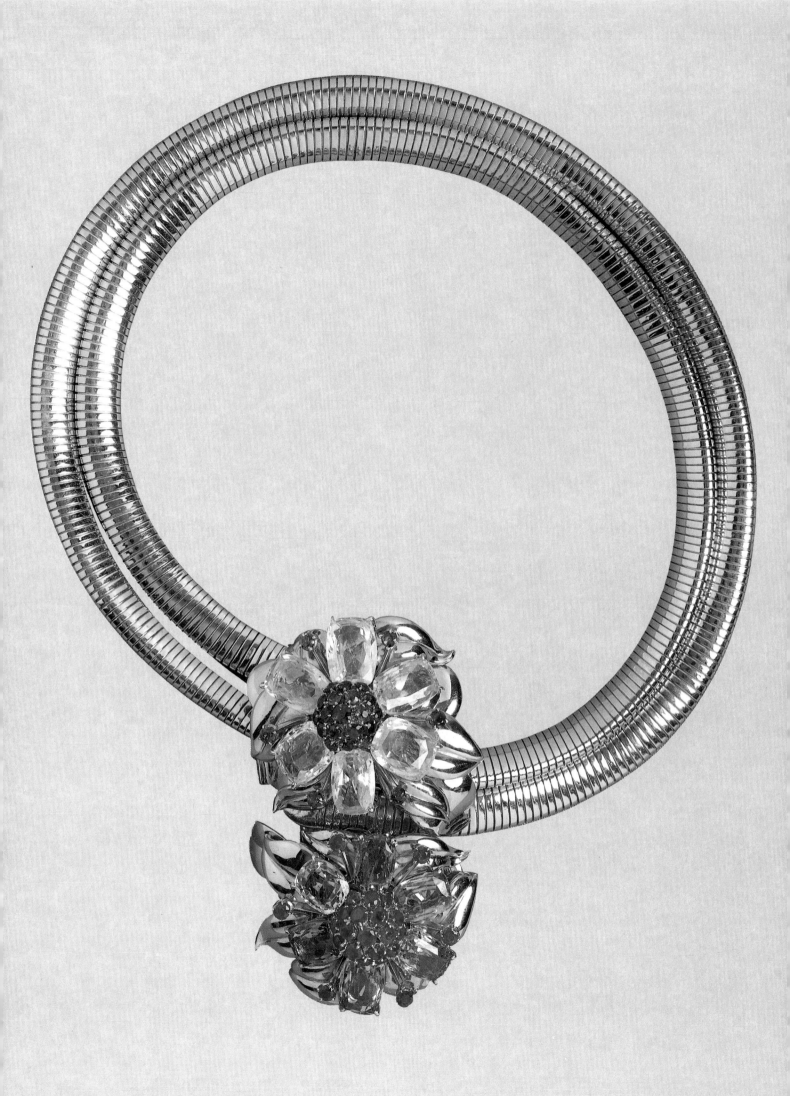

Four gouache designs for bracelets of baguette, trapezoidal and square diamonds, with a ground of brilliants mounted in platinum, circa 1938. Enlargement.

Preceding page, left: Serpent chain necklace in gold, with a "Passepartout" clip consisting of two flowers of yellow and blue faceted Ceylon sapphires and rubies, 1939. Enlargement.

Preceding page, right: "Posy" clip in yellow and blue Ceylon sapphires, round rubies and round faceted sapphires, with leaves and stems of polished gold, 1939. Enlargement.

"Costume jewelry" bracelet composed of short batons of engraved ivory with coral beads at each end, mounted on gold, 1931. Private collection, New York.

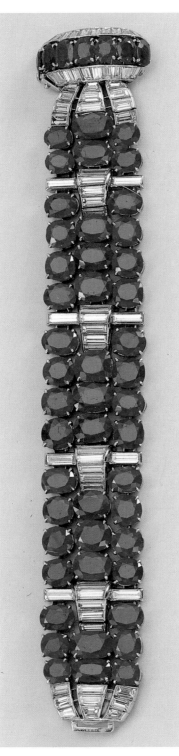

Bracelet of baguette diamonds and oval faceted rubies in platinum, 1937. Private collection.

Chain bracelet of polished gold with serti étoilé sapphires, circa 1938. Private collection. Photograph by Laurent Sully Jaulmes.

Gouache of two "Peony" clips in serti invisible *rubies and faceted rubies in gold, stems in diamonds and leaves of brilliants in platinum, which could be combined and worn as a corsage ornament, 1936.*

Facing page: "Peony" clip in serti invisible *rubies and faceted rubies in gold, leaves of brilliants and stems of baguette diamonds in platinum, 1936. Van Cleef & Arpels collection. Enlargement.*

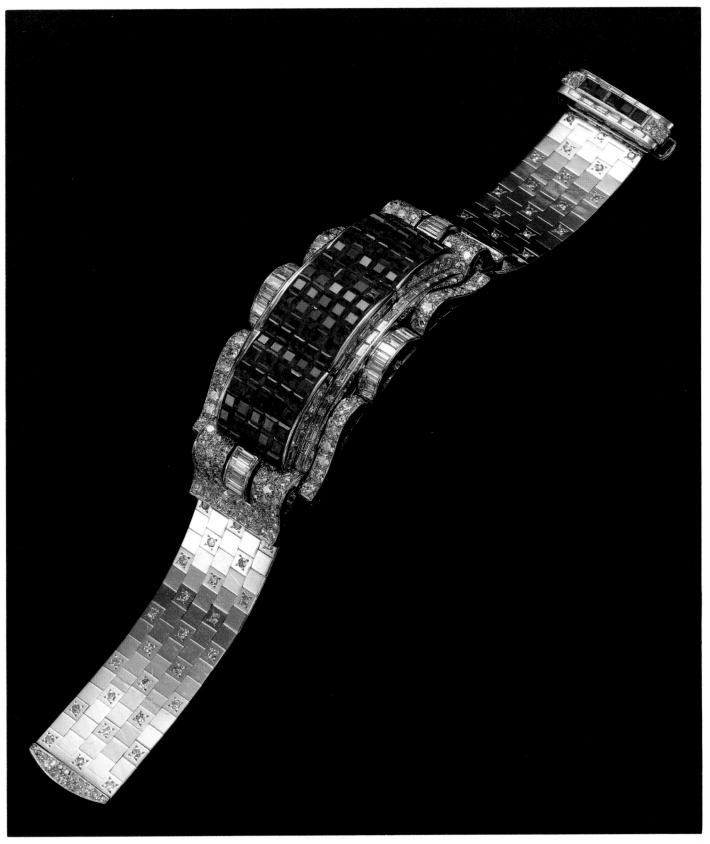

Platinum "Ludo" *bracelet with a central motif made up of three arches in* serti invisible *rubies surrounded by baguette diamonds and brilliants, circa 1930. This bracelet was knocked down at 18,000 dollars at Sotheby's New York in December 1984.*

Facing page: "Rose" *brooch with twenty-five petals in* serti invisible *rubies on gold, two leaves in* serti invisible *emeralds on gold and veins of diamonds in platinum; 614 rubies and 241 emeralds, 1938. Court of Egypt.*

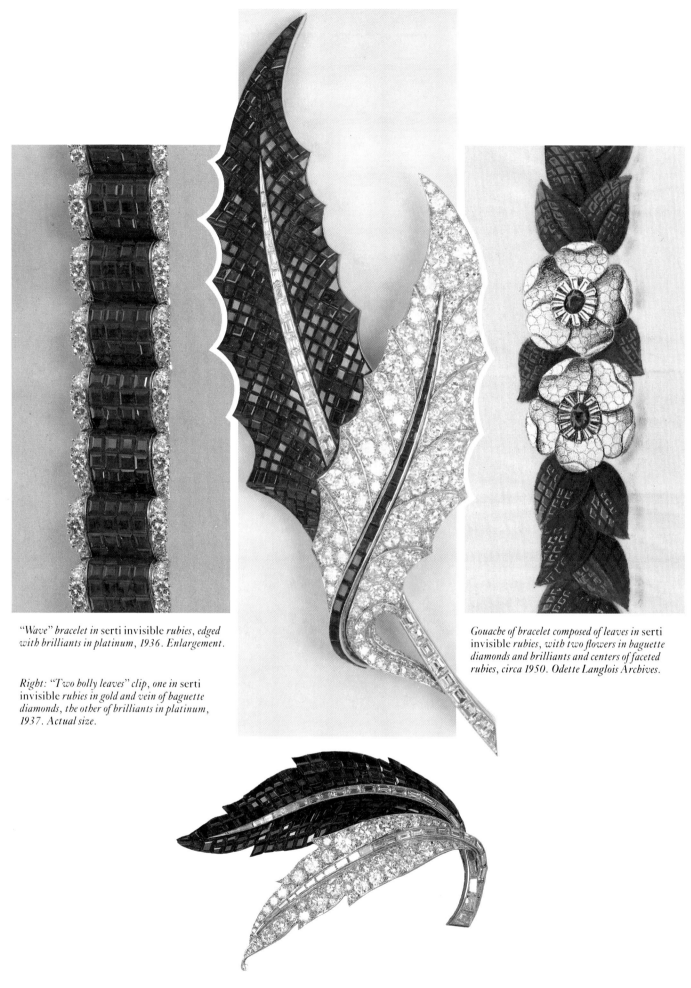

"Wave" bracelet in serti invisible *rubies, edged with brilliants in platinum, 1936. Enlargement.*

Right: "Two holly leaves" clip, one in serti invisible *rubies in gold and vein of baguette diamonds, the other of brilliants in platinum, 1937. Actual size.*

Gouache of bracelet composed of leaves in serti invisible *rubies, with two flowers in baguette diamonds and brilliants and centers of faceted rubies, circa 1950. Odette Langlois Archives.*

"Two leaves" clip, one in serti invisible *sapphires, the other of brilliants; the stems and veins are of baguette diamonds in platinum, 1965. Enlargement.*

Above and far right: Two gouaches by René-Sim Lacaze: projects for a necklace commissioned by the Duchess of Windsor in oval faceted rubies and baguette diamonds on platinum, 1938. René-Sim Lacaze collection.

Left: The Duchess of Windsor wearing the ruby necklace made at her request from a project by René-Sim Lacaze, a "holly leaves" double clip in serti invisible rubies and diamonds in her hair, and an "ivy leaf" earring in serti invisible rubies and diamonds.

"Two holly leaves" brooch in serti invisible rubies on gold and baguette diamonds in platinum, 1937. Enlargement.

"Poppy" clip with petals in serti invisible *sapphires, center and leaf in brilliants and stem of baguette diamonds, mounted in platinum, 1970. Enlargement.*

Bracelet in serti invisible *rubies or* serti invisible *sapphires, edged with baguette diamonds, circa 1940. Enlargement.*

"Poppy" earrings with petals in serti invisible *sapphires and center in brilliants, 1970. Enlargement.*

208

"Butterfly" clip in serti invisible *sapphires, navette diamonds
and brilliants in platinum, 1973. Enlargement.*

*Following page, left: "Serpent chain" with flowing motif in gold
and brilliants on platinum and two beads encrusted with* serti
étoilé *brilliants, 1948. Earrings in gold encrusted with
brilliants, 1948. Lewis M. Kaplan Gallery, London. Enlargement.*

*Following page, right: "Serpent chain" necklace with finials set
with brilliants on platinum and a flexible tassel with gold beads
encrusted with* serti étoilé *brilliants, 1943. Private collection.
Photograph by Laurent Sully Jaulmes. Enlargement.*

Gouache designs for signet rings bearing Renée Puissant's signature, made at the beginning of the thirties: a signet ring with a diamond set in platinum; a signet ring with a hexagonal cabochon emerald, surrounded by baguette diamonds, mounted in platinum.

Ring in polished gold, fluted body with two Ceylon sapphires, one blue, the other yellow, 1944. Van Cleef & Arpels collection. Enlargement.

Ring in polished gold and calibré *sapphires, 1936. Private collection, Paris. Enlargement.*

Facing page: Necklace made up of three gold serpent chains, knotted, decorated with cabochon sapphires and brilliants in platinum, with matching bracelet, 1949. Enlargement.

Gouache designs for signet rings bearing Renée Puissant's signature, made at the beginning of the thirties: a signet ring with an oval cabochon emerald and baguette diamonds, mounted in platinum. Atelier Ehret collection. Signet ring with an emerald-cut diamond surrounded by baguette diamonds mounted in platinum.

"Lace bouquet" in polished, pierced gold, faceted rubies, Ceylon sapphires and brilliants, 1947. Van Cleef & Arpels collection. Enlargement.

Facing page: "Résille" (lattice) bracelet in polished, pierced gold, brilliants, faceted and cabochon rubies, with a "serpent chain" clasp in gold, 1946. Enlargement.

*Bracelet in gold tulle with "Hawaii" flowers in faceted sapphires
and rubies and brilliants, with matching earrings and clips,
1942. Private collection. Enlargement.*

Advertisement which appeared in the magazine "Femme Chic" in October 1942. The model is wearing a dress by Marcella Alix and a hat by Albouy.

Following page, left: "Lace bow" clip in polished, pierced gold, white enamel, rubies and brilliants, 1949. Private collection. Enlargement.

Following page, right: "Dancer" clips: the head is a pear-shaped brilliant or a rose-cut diamond edged with rubies and emeralds, the torso is covered in diamonds set à grain and the skirts are made up of rose-cut diamonds, and small emeralds and rubies on bezels, 1943–1944. Enlargement. Private collection, New York.

Model wearing a necklace with a detachable clip derived from the gerbe (sheaf) motif and a "Sévigné" bracelet in twisted gold threads and brilliants. Photo taken at the beginning of the fifties.

Top: "Cascade" clip of baguette and navette diamonds and brilliants mounted in platinum, circa 1952. Van Cleef & Arpels collection.

Left: "Volutes" bracelet of pear-shaped and baguette diamonds, mounted in platinum, 1954. Enlargement.

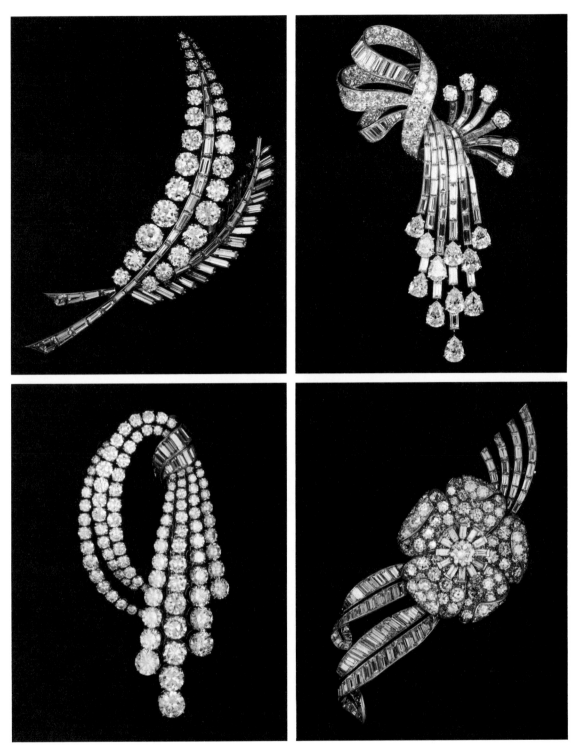

"Epis" (ears of corn) of baguette diamonds and
brilliants in platinum, 1956.

Clip of baguette diamonds and brilliants in
platinum, which could be worn on a necklace of
brilliants, 1949.

"Rain" clip of pear-shaped and baguette diamonds
and brilliants in platinum, 1951.

Flower clip of baguette diamonds and brilliants in
platinum, 1956.

Above left: "Garland" clip of pear-shaped and baguette diamonds and pear-shaped faceted sapphires, in platinum, 1961. Enlargement.

Above right: "Garland" clip of navette and baguette diamonds, brilliants and round faceted rubies in platinum, 1960. Enlargement.

Left: "Garland" clip of pear-shaped and baguette diamonds and brilliants, pear-shaped and round faceted rubies in platinum, 1959. Enlargement.

Double clip of baguette diamonds, brilliants, emerald-cut and oval faceted rubies, which could be worn separately or be attached to a bracelet or an osmior serpent chain, 1939. Enlargement. Private collection.

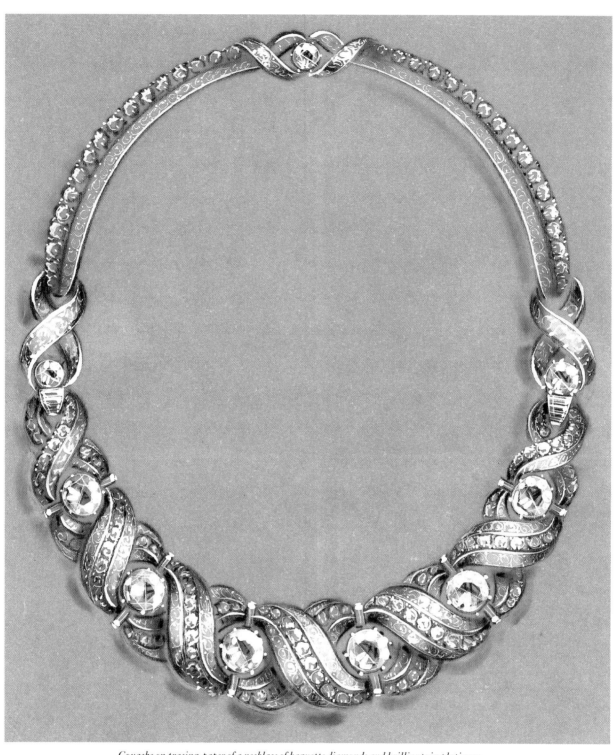

*Gouache on tracing-paper of a necklace of baguette diamonds and brilliants in platinum.
It was one of the projects executed in 1950 at the request of Her Royal Highness Princess
Fawzia of Egypt. Enlargement.*

Gouache on tracing-paper of a necklace made up of three rows of brilliants with a central voluted motif and six brilliants suspended from this, mounted in platinum. It was one of the projects executed in 1955 at the request of Her Royal Highness Princess Fawzia of Egypt. Enlargement.

Model wearing a "Passepartout" clip in the form of a bow, attached to a serpent chain with a matching bracelet. The coat has "Bee" clips pinned on to it, circa 1948.

Facing page: "Alvéoles" (honeycomb) bracelet in polished gold with three detachable "Bee" clips in gold brilliants, cabochon rubies and blue Ceylon sapphires, 1947. Private collection. Enlargement.

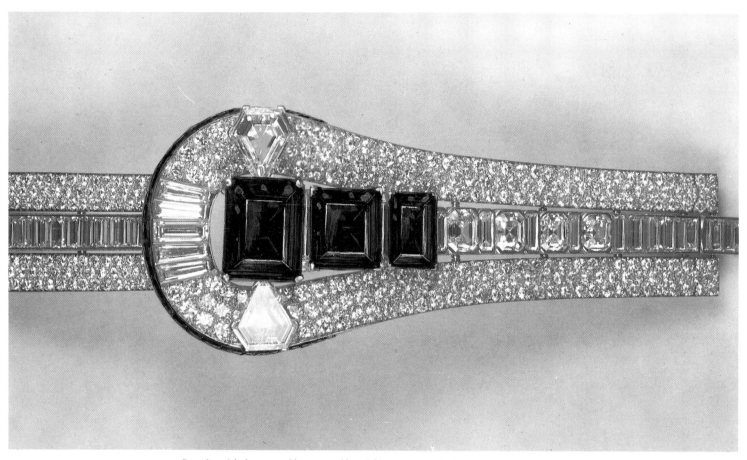

Bracelet with three emerald-cut emeralds weighing 20.21 carats, 10.58 carats and 6.38 carats, baguette emeralds, emerald-cut and baguette diamonds with a ground of brilliants, mounted in platinum, made in 1941 in New York. Enlargement.

Specially commissioned necklace with nine brilliants weighing approximately 85 carats, suspended from leaf motifs in gold arranged in chevrons, 1952.

"Cravat" necklace of baguette diamonds, brilliants and oval faceted sapphires in platinum, 1954. Enlargement.

Following page, left: "Cavalry" clip in gold set with calibré rubies and brilliants, 1943. Private collection, Paris. Enlargement.

Following page, right: "Ressort" (coil) bracelet in gold with a "Cadénas" (padlock) clasp with calibré rubies, serti étoilé brilliants, made in New York at the beginning of the forties. Private collection, Paris. Enlargement.

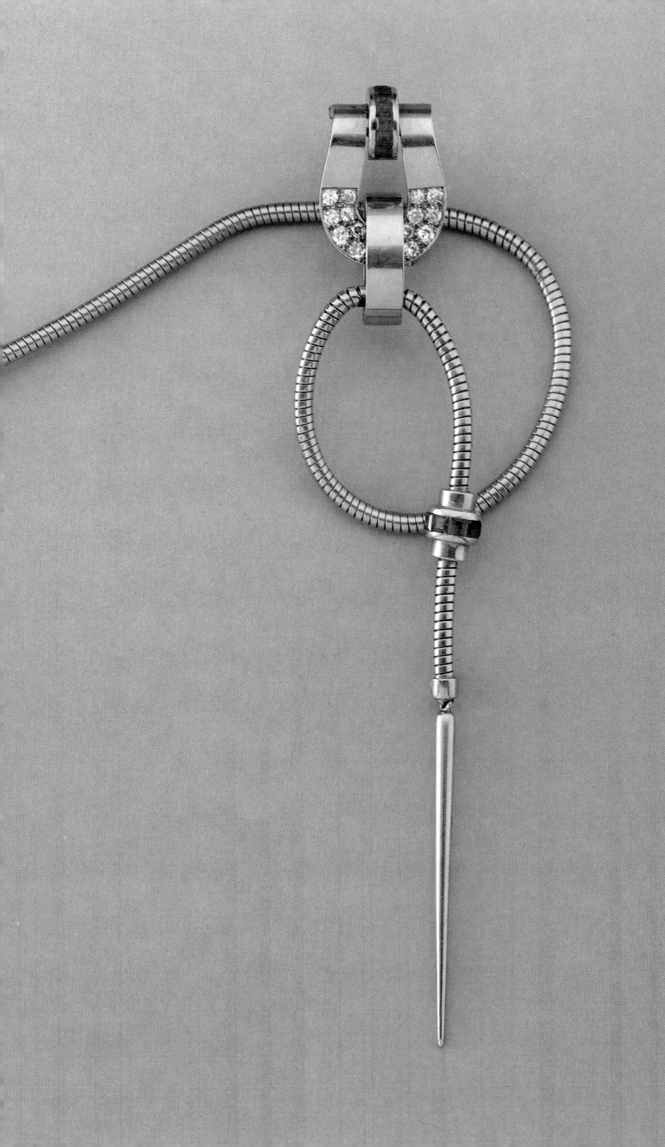

Necklace with three pear-shaped diamonds weighing 21.55 carats, baguette and navette diamond and brilliants in platinum, 1956.

Necklace comprising a line of baguette diamonds from which are suspended pear-shaped diamonds—the seven largest weighing 96.30 carats—baguette diamonds and brilliants on platinum, 1957.

"Clover" necklace in pear-shaped and navette diamonds and brilliants with a total weight of 130.79 carats. The central motif can be detached and worn as a clip and the necklace worn as a bracelet, 1959.

Necklace comprising nine pear-shaped diamonds of about 70 carats, baguette and navette diamonds and brilliants mounted on platinum, 1957. The necklace can also be worn as a tiara. Enlargement.

233

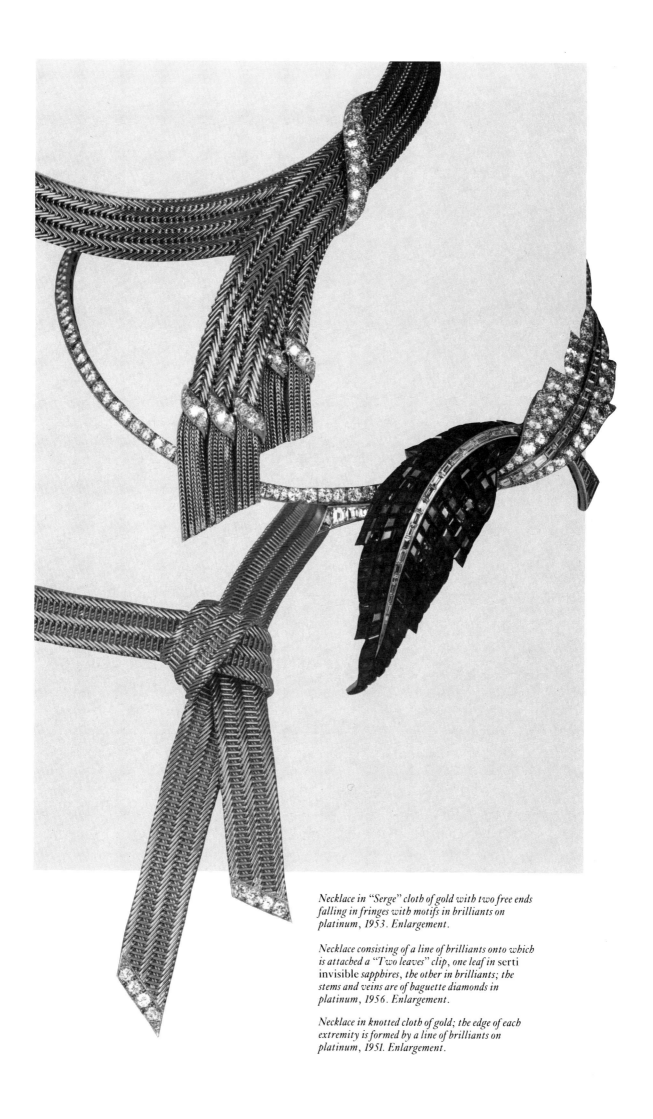

Necklace in "Serge" cloth of gold with two free ends falling in fringes with motifs in brilliants on platinum, 1953. Enlargement.

Necklace consisting of a line of brilliants onto which is attached a "Two leaves" clip, one leaf in serti invisible sapphires, the other in brilliants; the stems and veins are of baguette diamonds in platinum, 1956. Enlargement.

Necklace in knotted cloth of gold; the edge of each extremity is formed by a line of brilliants on platinum, 1951. Enlargement.

"Zip" necklace of flexible gold and brilliants. When the upper part of the necklace is removed, the piece can be worn, closed, as a bracelet and the pompom tassel then falls across the arm, 1951. Van Cleef & Arpels collection. Enlargement.

"Lawn" bracelet made up of gold beads and "Hawaii" flowers in gold, brilliants, and faceted rubies and sapphires, 1948. Enlargement.

Bracelet of pear-shaped and baguette diamonds and brilliants in platinum. The central ornament can be detached and worn as a clip, 1954.

Bracelet made up of alternate lines of oval faceted rubies, baguette diamonds and brilliants on platinum, 1956. Enlargement.

236

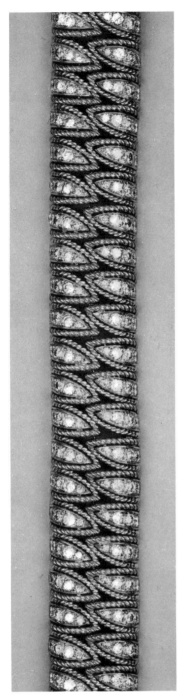

Bracelet of twisted gold thread
and brilliants set in platinum,
1959. Enlargement.

Bracelet of pear-shaped and
baguette diamonds and
brilliants in platinum. The
central flower can be detached
and worn as a clip, 1957.

Bracelet made up of flowers of
fluted gold, brilliants and
faceted emeralds and sapphires,
1954. Enlargement.

237

Bracelet of polished gold with a bead motif in faceted rubies, circa 1940. Private collection, Paris. Photograph by Laurent Sully Jaulmes. Enlargement.

Facing page: "Cavalry" clip comprising a flexible gold chain and articulated pendants composed of polished gold spangles and brilliants, 1943. Private collection, Paris. Photograph by Laurent Sully Jaulmes. Enlargement.

*"Kodak" earrings comprising
falling motifs in faceted
sapphires and brilliants in
platinum, 1968.*

*Earrings with three
aquamarines edged with a
double row of twisted gold
thread, set off with three
brilliants, 1963.*

*"Flower" earrings with petals
in* serti invisible *sapphires in
gold, edged with brilliants and
with centers of brilliants in
platinum, 1973.
Enlargement.*

*Earrings comprising an oval
faceted sapphire surrounded by
round faceted rubies and
emeralds in gold, with a tassel
fringe in gold threads, designed
to be worn with the "Zip"
necklace of precious stones,
1949.*

*"Flower" earrings with the
center formed by an oval
faceted sapphire, the petals of
sapphires cut to fit and edged
with brilliants, mounted in
platinum, 1966.*

*"Flower" earrings with petals
in* serti invisible *rubies in
gold, edged with brilliants and
with the center of brilliants in
platinum with a tassel hanging
down of brilliants and* serti
invisible *rubies, 1969. Van
Cleef & Arpels collection.
Enlargement.*

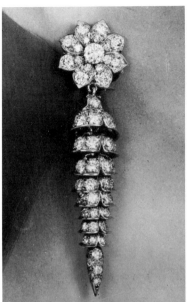

Pendant earrings in colored precious stone cabochons and brilliants in gold.

Pendant earrings in cabochon and ruby drops and brilliants mounted on gold, 1971.

Pendant earrings comprising a flower of brilliants from which an articulated, detachable ornament is hung, so that the flower can be worn on its own. Mounted in platinum, 1951.

Pendant earrings comprising a flower of brilliants and baguette diamonds from which a hanging motif of baguette and pear-shaped diamonds and brilliants in platinum is suspended, 1951.

Pendant earrings of baguette and navette diamonds in platinum, circa 1950.

Pendant earrings of baguette diamonds and faceted sapphires in platinum, circa 1936.

241

Necklace in the Indian mode comprising nine emerald drops, cabochon rubies and brilliants mounted in gold.

Necklace in the Indian mode comprising thirty-one emeralds, thirteen cabochon rubies and two hundred and thirty-four brilliants mounted in gold. It was made in 1954 for the Maharanee of Baroda.

243

Model wearing pendant earrings of gold, pear-shaped diamonds and brilliants mounted in gold; a necklace of navette, pear-shaped, briolette diamonds and antique-cut brilliants mounted in gold from which hangs a "Paiva" pendant clip comprising an antique-cut diamond surrounded by brilliants, pear-shaped, navette and briolette diamonds mounted in gold; and a ring with an antique-cut diamond surrounded by navette diamonds, 1966.

Drop pendant earrings of pear-shaped, baguette and navette diamonds in platinum,
1957. Enlargement.

Pendant earrings of navette diamonds and brilliants, circa 1960. Enlargement.

Gold bracelet with three beads set with turquoises and strewn with little flowers of rubies and brilliants, circa 1955. Primavera Gallery, New York. Enlargement.

Following page: Necklace of brilliants, rubies, emeralds and cabochon sapphires edged with twisted gold thread, circa 1955. Private collection. Enlargement.

"Serre-chignon" *tiara with swan in brilliants. The swan can be detached and worn as*
a clip; the bandeau in brilliants can be worn as a bracelet: mounted in platinum, 1965.
It was worn by Princess Grace of Monaco.

Tiara made up of seventeen pear-shaped diamonds, navette diamonds and brilliants
mounted in platinum which can also be worn as a necklace. On 28 June 1978 it was
worn by Princess Grace of Monaco at the wedding of her daughter, Princess Caroline.
Van Cleef & Arpels collection.

Pendant and chain made up of oval concentric rings in brilliants on gold, 1976.

Pendant and chain in gold and brilliants: the pendant is in the form of a lion's head in brilliants with pear-shaped faceted emerald eyes, holding in its mouth a ring in brilliants, on gold, 1974.

Pendant and chain in brilliants arranged in oval festoons, fausse-poires *and* fausse-navettes *in brilliants in gold, 1977.*

249

Necklace of oval faceted rubies and pear-shaped diamonds with a detachable pendant of oval faceted rubies surrounded by brilliants and pear-shaped diamonds, set in platinum. The necklace can be worn as a bracelet, 1966. Enlargement.

Facing page: "Natte" (plait) bracelet of brilliants and faceted rubies in platinum, 1963. Enlargement.

Necklace comprising nine emerald drops, with a total weight of 60.93 carats, hung from brilliants and baguette diamonds set in gold, 1982. Enlargement.

Necklace with pendant comprising eight emerald-cut emeralds with a total weight of 34.01 carats, mounted in gold, surrounded by navette diamonds and brilliants in platinum. This necklace can be adapted and worn as a bracelet, 1960. Enlargement.

Sautoir *in oval diamonds from which hangs a pendant with an exceptional faceted emerald of 53.85 carats surrounded by brilliants and pear-shaped diamonds, mounted in platinum, 1975. Enlargement.*

Necklace with seven oval faceted rubies of 24 carats and brilliants mounted in gold; thanks to a special armature, it can be worn as a tiara, 1985. Enlargement.

Necklace with three cushion-cut diamonds, with a total weight of 13.86 carats, surrounded by brilliants and antique-cut diamonds, mounted in gold, 1986. Enlargement.

Facing page: Bracelet made up of four rows of serti invisible rubies, two hundred and thirty six in all, edged on either side by a row of brilliants, a hundred and seventy-eight in all, circa 1980. Enlargement.

Sautoir made up of pear-shaped and navette diamonds from which hangs an incomparable sapphire of 139 carats and a pear-shaped sapphire of 118 carats, edged with a double row of brilliants, 1973.

Accessories

VANITY CASES

Van Cleef & Arpels have brought their reputation to bear on the art of the lady's *nécessaire*, termed 'vanity case' by the Americans. This accessory was one of the most extraordinary items produced after the First World War. These unique pieces, infinitely various in form and decoration, all contained, within a confined space, a powder compact, lipstick, tortoise-shell comb, mirror and sometimes even a little ivory note card and pencil, reminiscent of the former *carnet de bal*. Often inspired by inro, the curious little box with horizontal drawers in which the Chinese and Japanese used to carry their patent remedies, they might be flat and rectangular, oval or cylindrical, and were sometimes attached to an onyx ring or a lipstick case by a silk cord, thus forming a handle.

Their surface decoration might be starkly plain or covered with figurative scenes, veritable miniature pictures in gems and hard stones, demonstrating a staggering mastery of jewelry techniques. The abundance of materials associated with these vanity cases gives one an inkling of the extraordinary range of possibilities open to the artists: precious stones, enamel in every shade (sometimes used to imitate marble), lapis lazuli, amethyst, coral, turquoise, nephrite, jasper, chrysoprase, mauve, blue, green, pink or white jade, grey, green or pink agate, aventurine (spangled green), green veined malachite, burnt yellow topaz (either light or dark), citrine, cornelian, transparent or frosted rock crystal, amber, tortoise-shell, wood, moonstone, sunstone, mother-of-pearl, amazonite, sodalite, rose quartz, cat's eye, labradorite, ivory, *oeuil de faucon*, and so on.

The artists played with the beguiling possibilities of all these stones, producing, on the one hand, a startling and sharply contrasted polychromy inspired by the Ballets Russes, which had such a great influence on art between 1910 and 1920, or, on the other hand, choosing materials which allowed them to produce the most delicate cameos and the most subtle harmonic effects worthy of the refinements of Persian art.

As with all jewelry produced at this time, the art of distant exotic civilizations—China, Japan, Persia—exerted a powerful influence. The creators freely interpreted ornamental motifs and figurative scenes from those countries. From China they retained symbolic signs, landscapes, dragons, clouds, Buddhas and enamelled flowers, used as repetitive motifs, either juxtaposed or interlaced.

In 1926, for example, a very elongated rectangular vanity case with an amber plaque framed in black enamel bore at its center the Chinese good luck symbol, the Shou, which both protects and ensures longevity. Two friezes of symbolic signs—rolls of thunder and bands of clouds—extend across the circumference of the box which terminates, at one end, in a mandarin's hat turned up into a pagoda roof (in rose-cut diamonds surmounted by an emerald cabochon) and, at the other, in an engraved amber flower with a cabochon emerald center.

Another vanity case, cylindrical in shape, made in 1924 (in red and black enamel decorated with jade flowers in the Chinese style with coral pistils and rose-cut diamond leaves on platinum), was attached by a chain to an onyx ring. The same year, another model in black enamel and jade bore as its central decoration a disc depicting passing clouds.

Japan also provided inspiration to Van Cleef & Arpels and numerous models in black enamel were enhanced by central bands of chrysanthemums or peonies in pastel shades composed of mother-of-pearl inlay, suggesting the delicate fabrics of traditional ceremonial robes. Sometimes, for example, cherry blossom in green jade and rose-cut diamonds was set against a background of red enamel edged with black. A unique model created in 1927 harked back to Japanese prints; it depicted a temple in the shade of a tree, by the sea shore, under a clouded sky in delicate mother-of-pearl inlay with blue tones, edged with sky-blue and black enamel and with rose-cut diamond corner-pieces.

Yet other vanity cases had a Persian inspiration. Sumptuous

Drawing of an elongated Art Deco vanity case comprising an amber plaque framed in black enamel, with the Chinese good-luck "Shou" symbol at its center, signifying protection and longevity. Two friezes of symbolic signs—thunder rolls and bands of clouds—run round the circumference of the box which, at one end, becomes a mandarin's hat turned up into a pagoda roof of rose-cut diamonds, topped with an emerald cabochon, and at the other a flower in engraved amber with an emerald cabochon center, 1926.

261

mother-of-pearl mosaics reproduced motifs from ceramic floor and wall tiles, or from carpets with geometric or figurative subjects (rhombs, delicate arabesques, interlaced patterns, stylized birds and flowers), all executed in the softest and most subtle colors.

The lacquerwork and mother-of-pearl inlay produced in the twenties is worthy of comparison with work produced in ancient times. Vladimir Makowsky (1884–1966), a Russian artist who established himself in Paris after making numerous journeys to the Far East, was responsible for some of the House's most astonishing vanity cases. One of his models, created in 1926, was a composition inspired by the Middle Ages. In mother-of-pearl inlay in gold, black, blue and red enamel, it depicted three arches in engraved gold separated by colonnettes framing three armed warriors on horseback, in profile. This tryptich, punctuated diagonally by the lances, the swords and the horses' legs, is edged with a double fillet of black enamel and rose-cut diamonds, broken by four symmetrical chevron motifs in blue enamel and brilliants. Comparable in splendor is another model, created the same year by Aronsberg, also recalling the Middle Ages. It represents a Romano-Byzantine window—two colonnettes supporting an arch in sculpted black onyx, encrusted with geometric friezes in rose-cut diamonds—beyond which is seen a landscape in enamel, gold and engraved mother-of-pearl mosaic in infinitely subtle shades of green, blue, pink and mauve; in the middle of the landscape a horseman sits, dressed in a cape of blue diamonds, half-hidden behind his shield of blue enamel set off with gold lions, brandishing a sword.

Also in 1926, a hunting scene set against the background of a Medieval chateau was executed in gold, mother-of-pearl inlay and enamel, edged with black enamel and embellished with rose-cut diamond motifs. There were other vanity cases which took up themes from this period, such as the Bayeux Tapestry, griffins, *millefleurs*, and unicorns.

The fascination with ornamental motifs drawn from distant civilizations or our own European past did not prevent the creators

Drawing of an Art Deco vanity case created in 1926 by Aronsberg: it depicts a Romano-Byzantine window frame—two colonnettes supporting an arch in black sculpted onyx, encrusted with geometric friezes in rose-cut diamonds—through which is seen a landscape in enamel, gold and a mosaic of engraved mother-of-pearl in the midst of which a warrior stands.

from exercising their talents on a variety of contemporary themes, particularly those of interior design with its stylized floral motifs, created by designers such as Follot, Sue and Mare, and Benedictus for fabrics, wallpapers or wrought iron work. For example, there were several vanity cases decorated with enamelled or engraved flowers, set with precious or semi-precious stones arranged in garlands, ribbons, or bouquets, in round central motifs or in rhombs against a crystal or onyx background, disposed in semi-circles, in symmetrical or asymmetrical triangles, or again framing a tiered fountain from which water flows in long threads, or in rose-cut diamond icicles, the very quintessence of Art Deco.

The inside of an Art Deco vanity case in gold and blue enamel, 1928.

Drawing of an Art Deco vanity case depicting a tiered fountain from which water flows in long streams, or icicles, made in gold, black enamel, lapis, jade and rose-cut diamonds, 1926.

Every attractive image provided a pretext for a new ornamental design. In 1924, a model in black enamel edged with green bore three elephants in Indian file, formed of rose-cut diamonds, arranged in decreasing size, one behind the other, in profile. Alongside the images borrowed from flora or fauna, the multiple possibilities offered by geometric forms were exploited: triangles, rhombs and circles were arranged into ornamental borders or spread across the whole surface. When executed in polychrome enamel, they might reveal the harmony of subtle shades or the boldness of violent contrasts. Sometimes these geometric figures were accented by baguette diamonds which striped the surface with flashes of light, and opaque or translucent *cloisonné* enamel was used to imitate the aspect of precious stones. Certain models reconciled the two principal themes of Art Deco, figuration and geometry, and even played with their complementarity. The objects incorporating these artistic innovations could, for the most part, compare with the most precious boxes of the eighteenth century, the most obvious references in this field, and were executed in the Strauss, Allard and Meyer and Langlois workshops, where experienced craftsmen spent hundreds of hours manipulating materials chosen for their decorative qualities.

Art Deco vanity case in black enamel with rose-cut diamond ornaments framing a hunting scene inspired by the Middle Ages, made by Aronsberg in mother-of-pearl inlay, 1926. Private collection, New York.

Art Deco vanity case inspired by Japanese prints: it depicts a temple in the shade of a tree, by the seashore, under a cloudy sky and was made by Vladimir Makowsky in delicate bluish mother-of-pearl inlay, edged with sky-blue and black enamel with Chinese corner-pieces in rose-cut diamonds, 1925. Enlargement. Private collection, New York.

Art Deco vanity case in gold with flowers in crystal, onyx, moonstones, sapphires, with a central band of flowers in engraved lapis, edged with black enamel and rose-cut diamonds, 1925. Private collection.

Art Deco powder compact in polished lapis with floral motifs in engraved lapis and brilliants edged with fluted rock crystal, and with turquoise cabochons and brilliants on platinum, 1928. Private collection, New York.

Art Deco vanity case in yellow and white gold with flowers in semi-precious stones on a crystal plaque, edged with a double border of rose-cut diamonds and enamel imitating lapis, 1925. Private collection, New York.

*Art Deco cigarette case in jade, crystal, onyx and diamonds with a floral motif in
engraved lapis, 1928. Enlargement. Private collection, New York.*

Art Deco cigarette case decorated on both sides in gold and enamel imitating lapis, with a central band depicting a peacock in blue and green enamel on a pale green mosaic ground, 1925. Enlargement. Private collection, New York.

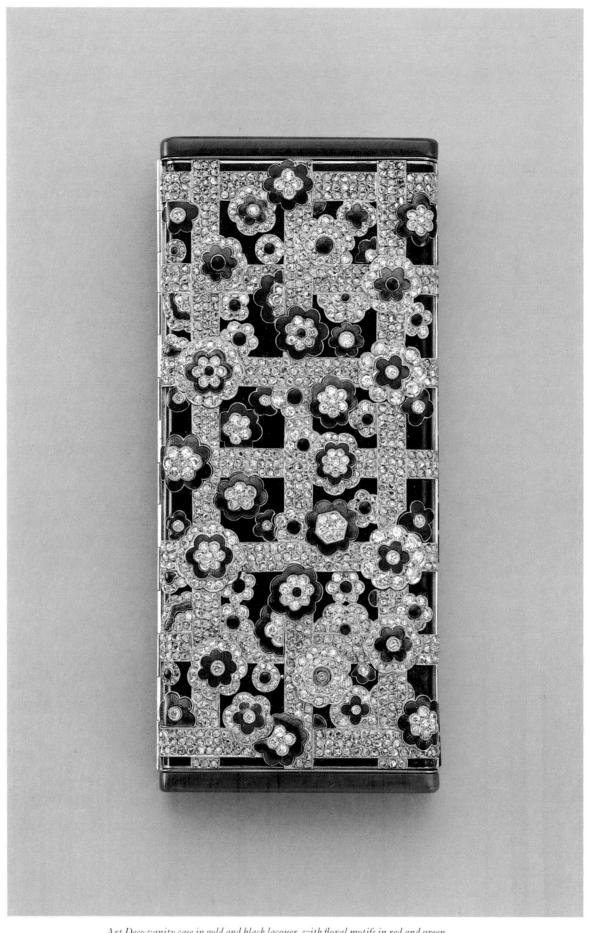

Art Deco vanity case in gold and black lacquer, with floral motifs in red and green enamel, and rose-cut diamonds on white gold, 1925. Enlargement. Actual size: 450 × 950 mm. Van Cleef & Arpels collection.

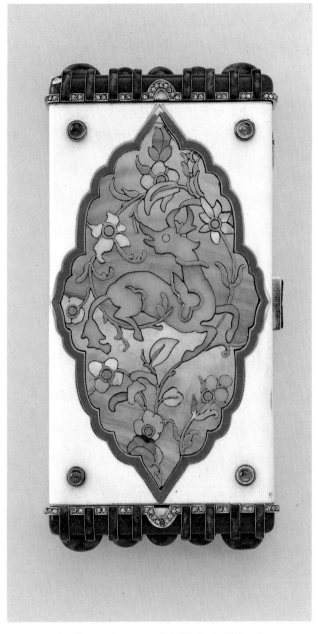

*Art Deco vanity case in mauve jade with flowers in
rose-cut diamonds, rubies and emeralds cut to fit,
edged with green and black enamel and rows of
rose-cut diamonds, 1926. Enlargement. Van Cleef
& Arpels collection.*

*Art Deco vanity case made by Vladimir Makowsky
in ivory and gold with mother-of-pearl inlay, edged
with red enamel and blue enamel imitating lapis,
rose-cut diamonds and emerald cabochons, 1925.
Enlargement. Private collection.*

Art Deco vanity case in gold, black enamel and blue enamel imitating lapis with lines of baguette diamonds and rose-cut diamonds with floral motifs in enamel along the sides, 1925. Private collection, New York.

POWDER COMPACTS

The splendor of the vanity cases should not make us forget the beauty of the powder compacts. A remarkable collection, created between 1923 and 1925, took on the form of envelopes in black enamel with a line of brilliants, or were made in *guilloché* gold or gold edged with black, green or white enamel; some were attached by a chain to a lipstick case. We should also mention some extraordinary pill boxes, created between 1925 and 1930, in osmior or grey gold that might be *guilloché* or engraved with geometric designs, embellished with a line of *calibré* colored precious stones; or again in enamel and hard stones with the inside of the lid decorated with enamelled scenes, anecdotic or exotic—penguins on an ice-floe, a seashore or rural landscape, or a pagoda with Mount Fujiyama in the background.

Cigarette cases, for their part, were made in every imaginable combination of gold, enamel and precious or hard stones. For example, a model of 1923, in red enamel on gold, had its extremities in jade decorated with rose-cut diamonds on platinum; the model also existed in *guilloché* gold with a chevron pattern. The following year, another model was made in red and green gold engraved with an interlaced pattern.

Drawing of the exterior and interior lid of a pillbox; on the inside of the lid penguins on an ice-floe are depicted, 1925–1930.

Drawing of an 'Envelope' Art Deco powder compact in gold and black and orange enamel, 1923–1925.

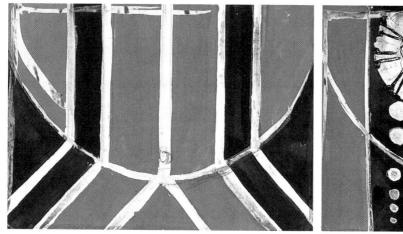 

Top and bottom: Three gouache designs for 'Envelope' powder compacts in red and black enamel, 1925.

Center: Art Deco 'Envelope' powder compact in gold and black and orange enamel, 1923. Van Cleef & Arpels collection.

HANDBAGS

The evening bags created by Van Cleef & Arpels between 1925 and 1930 achieved as much popularity as their vanity cases. Most were especially made for wealthy clients of that period. Fabrics and animal skins were chosen for their luxurious qualities or their rarity: spangled black satin, quilted silk, beige, black or crimson silk velvet, faille, brocades, beaded, ruched, gold-embroidered or braided fabrics, green or red piqué, suède, glazed kid, or beige, grey or blue antilope skin. Their frames and clasps in enamel and precious or hard stones had geometric or figurative motifs such as flowers or birds, often inspired by the East, and took on a whole variety of original forms (egg-shaped, pagoda-shaped, semi-hexagonal, trapezoidal). They had extraordinary buttons or clasps in the form of cabochons, figures, animals such as Egyptian cats in agate, obsidian, lapis, amethysts and crystal, Buddhas in amethysts, smoked agate and malachite, a standing dog in lapis, obsidian, crystal, turquoise and enamel, as well as strutting pigeons, lying or standing rabbits, elephants, mice, bears, swans, lions, scarabs, a Persian goddess seated in a shell, a Hindu goddess, a Billiken in agate or an odalisque whose body stretched right across the frame of the bag.

Art Deco evening bag with frame and clasp in platinum, onyx and brilliants, 1925.

275

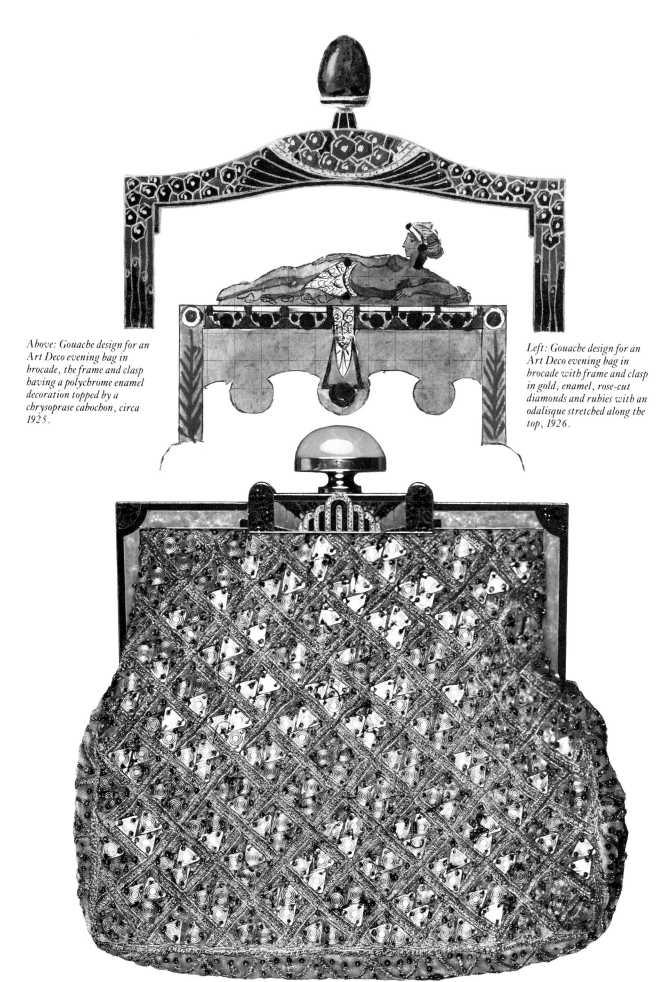

Above: Gouache design for an Art Deco evening bag in brocade, the frame and clasp having a polychrome enamel decoration topped by a chrysoprase cabochon, circa 1925.

Left: Gouache design for an Art Deco evening bag in brocade with frame and clasp in gold, enamel, rose-cut diamonds and rubies with an odalisque stretched along the top, 1926.

Evening bag in precious embroidered and sequined fabric, the frame and clasp having motifs in gold, enamel, platinum, rose-cut diamonds and a chrysoprase cabochon clasp, 1926. Van Cleef & Arpels collection.

After 1930, the vanity cases were taken one step further and developed into a larger box, termed the *minaudière* by Alfred Van Cleef, who patented the name as a tribute to his wife, Estelle, gently reproaching her for her tendancy to *minauder* (simper). The idea came to Charles Arpels on the occasion of a visit of one of his most loyal clients, Florence J. Gould, the wife of the American railroad magnate. Having come out in a hurry, she was using a large metal box (a large Lucky Strike cigarette box) that day as a handbag, and had thrown lipstick, compact, cigarette lighter and cigarettes pell-mell into it. Some months later, Charles Arpels introduced his own version of the ideal reticule, a fitting accessory for such an elegant woman. Henceforth, the *minaudière* replaced the evening bag or the dress bag carried in the afternoon. As it was generally made in a fabric to match a specific outfit or in a precious leather, elegant women were obliged to own several, each one selected to complement their most choice dresses. In gold or in lacquer (enamel was too fragile to be used on a large surface) *minaudières*, embellished with clasps consisting of pearls or precious stone cabochons, displayed their secrets thanks to ingenious mechanisms which revealed several compartments where powder, lipstick, minute gold pots filled with eye make-up, a comb, small change and cigarettes were to be found. Generally placed on one side, a special isolated compartment was reserved for a cigarette-holder and lighter. Certain *minaudières* incorporated a miniature watch, as in the "Domino" model which is still to be found in the Boutique des Heures.

From 1930 to the beginning of the sixties, *minaudières* were made in gold worked in various ways: fluted, engraved, chased, or gadrooned; depicting geometric or abstract motifs, draped fabric, waves, chevrons, basketwork, and radiating sun motifs. They recall the bookbindings of Legrain, Schmied and Rose Adler, but were enhanced with ornamental elements in rubies, *calibré* or cabochon sapphires arranged in bands, squares or rhombs, located centrally on the lid or arranged near the clasp. Certain models from the forties or fifties favored patterns composed of engraved or chased flowers or butterflies, scattered with precious stones. Often the motifs corresponded to *parures* in the House collections; for example, the model decorated with "Hawaii" flowers which was made the same year (1938) as the jewelry bearing that motif. For women who loved simplicity, luxurious models in black lacquer had a simple line of brilliants as their sole decoration. Clasps in gold and precious stones with abstract motifs—arcs and rods, multiple cones, volutes—or inspired by Chinese symbolic signs or again representing flowers or leaves, were often detachable and could be worn as clips. Some examples dating from 1936 will give an indication of their diversity and richness: a buttercup in brilliants with a pistil of oval emeralds and baguette diamonds; Colombian emerald leaves in *serti invisible*; a triple ivy leaf in precious stones. *Copeaux* (wood shavings), *volutes* (wreaths), or ribbons, *à pont* motifs in gold or in *serti invisible* were used for the most precious models. In 1939, Van Cleef & Arpels created a fantastic *minaudière* in polished yellow gold with a hummingbird on its lid, in *serti invisible* sapphires with a diamond eye, the bird poised over a branch in pink gold with ruby flowers in *serti invisible* and green gold leaves. Certain *minaudières*, marvels of virtuosity over which highly skilled craftsmen had worked for hundreds of hours, are quite unique pieces. One of these, however, met with a curious destiny when an Emir, who was passing through Paris some time in the sixties, chose a *minaudière* set with precious stones. He commissioned thirty absolutely identical copies so as not to provoke jealousy among the thirty wives in his harem.

Florence J. Gould, who inspired Van Cleef & Arpels to create the Minaudière *at the beginning of the thirties.*

Interior of a minaudière *with a radiating sun motif in polished and engraved gold, ornamented with a motif in* serti *invisible rubies, 1934. Actual size.*

Drawing by Don to celebrate the minaudière *created by Van Cleef & Arpels.*

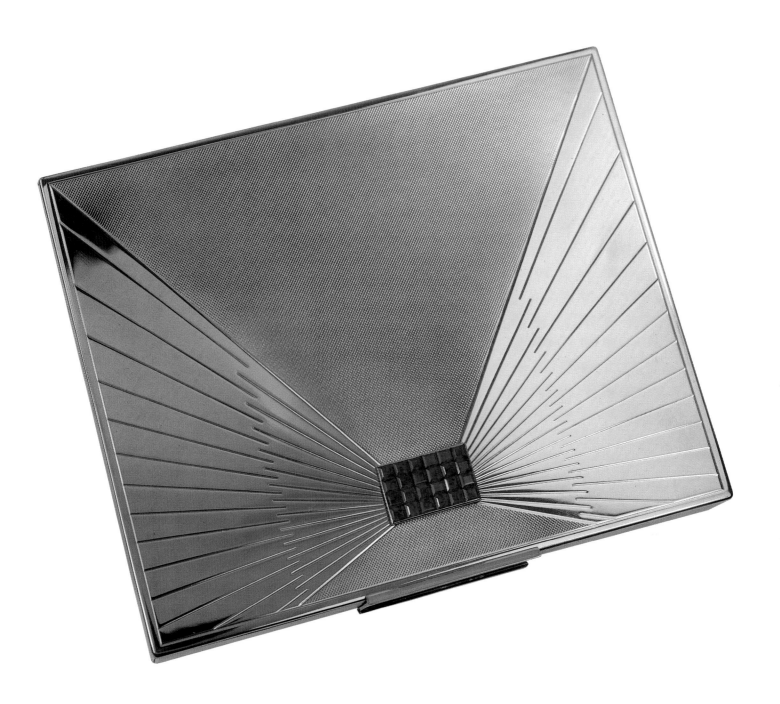

Minaudière *with a radiating sun motif in polished and engraved gold, and a motif in* serti invisible *rubies, 1934. Actual size. Van Cleef & Arpels collection.*

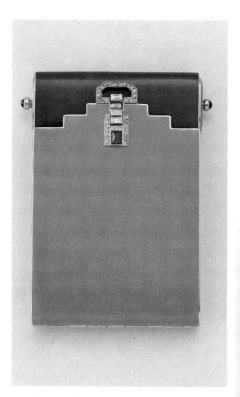

Art Deco powder compact in gold, pink and violet enamel, with a design in diamonds and cabochon sapphires, 1927. Van Cleef & Arpels collection.

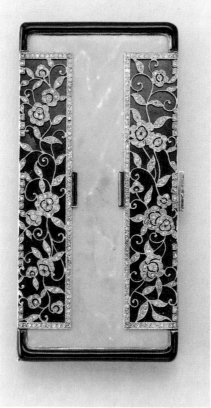

Art Deco vanity case in pink enamel imitating marble, with plaques of black enamel with flowers of rose-cut diamonds, edged with a line of gold and black enamel, 1925. Van Cleef & Arpels collection.

Art Deco powder compact in white enamel with coloured enamel flowers, enhanced with rose-cut diamonds at the sides, 1927. Van Cleef & Arpels collection.

Powder compact in black enamel and gold, with a border of baguette diamonds and brilliants on one side, 1933. Enlargement. Van Cleef & Arpels collection.

Art Deco powder compact in ribbed osmior with two lines of six calibré *rubies. The inside of the palladiated gold lid depicts an enamelled landscape, 1925–1930. Enlargement. Van Cleef & Arpels collection.*

Facing page: Reticule in polished engraved gold and black lacquer with marguerites in gold and rubies, with a gold serpent chain and platinum ring, 1949.

Cigarette case in polished gold with three pink flamingos in goutte de suif *rubies, onyx and emeralds cut to fit, 1939. Van Cleef & Arpels collection, Geneva.*

Powder compact in polished gold with a floral design in rubies and brilliants, 1951. Reduction. Van Cleef & Arpels collection.

Cigarette case in polished, engraved and chased gold, depicting a scene from a painting by Winterhalter, "Empress Eugénie and the ladies of her court," made in faceted diamonds, sapphires, emeralds and rubies, 1942. This cigarette case was the property of the Maharanee of Baroda. Reduction. Van Cleef & Arpels collection.

Cigarette case in polished gold, the lid decorated with a humming-bird in serti invisible *sapphires, with a diamond eye, poised over a branch in pink gold with flowers in* serti invisible *rubies and leaves in mat gold, 1938. Reduction. Van Cleef & Arpels collection.*

Drawing of an Art Deco cigarette case made in gold with a woven pattern in yellow, black and red enamel, 1927.

ACCESSORIES

The imagination of the House's creators was exercised also on all the indispensable accessories which an elegant woman of refined taste might slip into her handbag: her lipstick case, cigarette case, lighter, lip brush and mascara box were often decorated with the same ornamental motifs so that they would harmonize. For all these accessories, the designers and craftsmen worked gold in such a way as to give it a whole range of textures (gadrooned, woven, *guilloché*, chased) and colors (pink, green, yellow and grey, often combined on the same piece). For example, a cigarette case made in 1947 was executed in pink, green and palladiated gold, embellished by a clasp in brilliants; a compact in woven gold was studded with sapphires; and a shell compact was made in gold with a ruby clasp. For the numerous evening bags made in the forties and fifties, gold in all colors was woven to imitate basketwork, and was sometimes enhanced with a line of brilliants or colored gemstones.

Figurative motifs borrowed from the realm of flora or fauna were in great favor; flowers were scattered or arranged in bouquets, small leaves were worked in chevrons or butterflies, and there were those three pink flamingos in *calibré* rubies which adorned a cigarette case made in 1937. Among these creations, we might mention a few representative models which were made right up to the sixties: in the "47" collection (so called to commemorate the date of its creation), marguerites in yellow gold or platinum scattered with rubies, or still more butterflies, decorated *minaudières* and reticules as well as the accessories they contained. Another series depicted honeysuckle in gold and brilliants; in 1949, flowers in gold, called "Bagatelles," were encrusted on a silver and lacquer box. Some powder compacts were decorated with rural scenes—ducks swimming in a stream lined with trees under a sky across which some birds are flying. The most precious of all these powder compacts or cigarette cases were executed in *serti invisible*; one of these depicted a flying fish in rubies, its head set with brilliants, its tail and fins in gold, threading it way through emerald seaweed. For clients with the most refined tastes, ravishing pill boxes were clothed in rubies or sapphires in *serti invisible*. Certain special commissions were of the most eccentric kind; for example, in the twenties, Van Cleef & Arpels executed a pair of suspenders in gold, turquoise and brilliants.

Accessories for men were made more luxurious and were personalized: sumptuous motifs embellished cigarette cases; letter-holders became shields, horseshoes in wood or gold or trombones in

Pillbox in serti invisible *sapphires and polished gold, 1935. Van Cleef & Arpels collection.*

Clock lighter in guilloché *styptor and rolled gold, 1936.*

precious metal. Animal heads (foxes or dogs) appeared on tie-pins; shirt-studs were clothed in platinum and brilliants; cuff links became *bâtonnets* (small rods) of gold or precious stones in *serti invisible*; stirrup-pieces in gold and precious stones or plaques of gadrooned gold; leather wallets in the most subtle shades were engraved with geometric motifs recalling the bookbindings of Legrain or Schmied.

Elegant women, whose most insignificant accessory reflects their refinement, were not forgotten. Precious lorgnettes were created right up to the end of the twenties, as for example the model in

Art Deco cigarette cases in polished gold and black enamel, circa 1928.

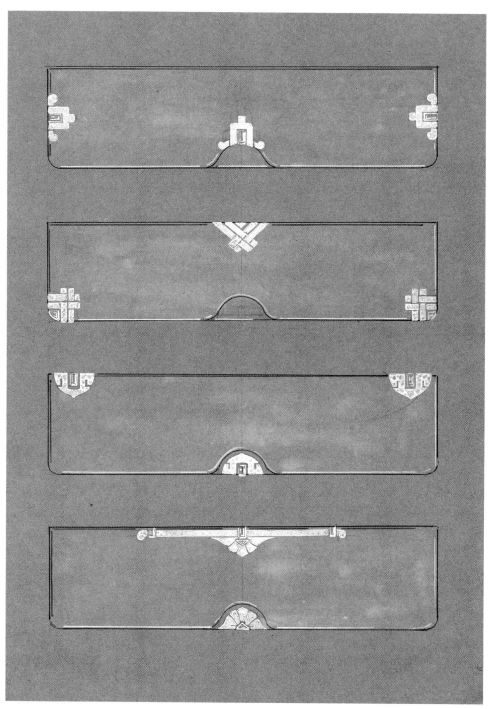

Page of drawings of tortoise-shell comb cases with diamonds motifs, 1920–1925.

black lacquer embellished with flowers and garlands set with rose-cut diamonds. Luxurious hair combs were devised at the same time for women who had not yet adopted the *coupe garçonne* or bobbed haircut. *Fantaisie* mirrors in green and black lacquer, onyx, rose quartz or nephrite were embellished with geometric motifs in gold and cabochon rubies. The most basic toilet articles were made in gold, as for example comb-cases which were decorated with flowers and birds in gold and precious or hard stones. Cigarette lighters were matched with powder compacts and cigarette cases.

Drawings of Art Deco hair combs in platinum, diamonds, emeralds and onyx, circa 1920.

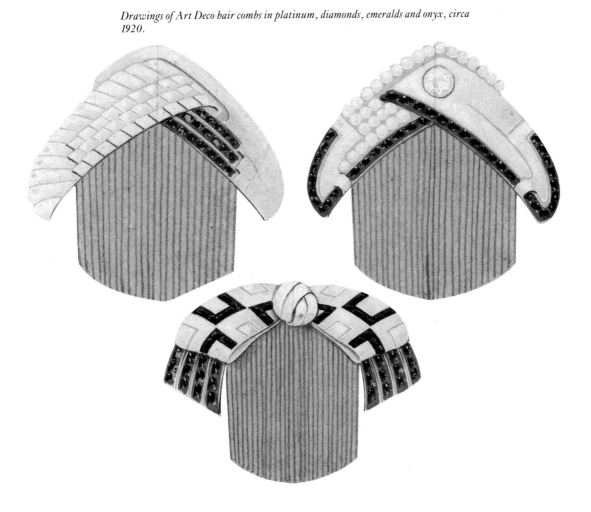

SPECIAL COMMISSIONS

Here we should not fail to mention those objects, sometimes useful, sometimes merely decorative, which were specially made to satisfy the mad whims of certain clients whose eccentricity had no bounds: desk sets in gold and precious stones; writing-pads in polychrome enamel; "Vendôme column" cigarette lighters; an extravagant lapis ashtray surmounted by a mauve jade Buddha embellished with moonstone cabochons and rose-cut diamonds; *pendulettes tournantes* (small turning clocks) whose back formed a photograph frame; a Bengalese bird cage in gold with a lapis base (the cage was commissioned by a maharajah who specified that it should contain a little gold ladder so that a *"reinette"* (tree frog) could be installed in the cage which, according to whether it climbed or descended the rungs, would indicate changes in the weather!); radiator caps in white rock crystal and a limousine canteen which were specially made for a German banker; suspenders composed of five hundred exquisite pearls; champagne swizzle sticks in platinum or toothpicks in precious metal; or a unique clock-snuffbox, bought in 1930 by the Duchess de Tallerand, for which the clock-dial was disguised in an ancient little Chinese sculpture, hollowed out to form a snuff-box.

Then, in 1984, the Marquis d'Aulan approached Van Cleef & Arpels and commissioned them to take a bottle of 1976 "Rare" and give it a gorgeous gold cladding to celebrate the 200th anniversary of the House of Piper-Hiedsieck. The idea of creating a "bottle-jewel" was greeted with enthusiasm by Van Cleef & Arpels. Seven artist-craftmen worked on the project and its execution occupied four months. They decided to cover the neck of the bottle with a mantle of gold tulle, to top it off with a real champagne cork-cage in double gold thread, and to encircle it with two rings of gold set with brilliants. The medallion consisted of gold scrolls and plaques of lapis lazuli studded with white gold, surrounding an area of chased black gold, encrusted with letters in relief in yellow gold.

A small clock is hidden inside this sculpted turquoise snuff-box which rests on a base of amethyst, 1928.

Solid silver fittings for a car, comprising a clock, a bar, a smoker's cabinet and so forth. Each compartment bears the letter "B," the first initial of the wife of the client for whom this commission was made.

*Cigarette case depicting the Place Vendôme, made in the fifties in
gold, diamonds, rubies and enamel.*

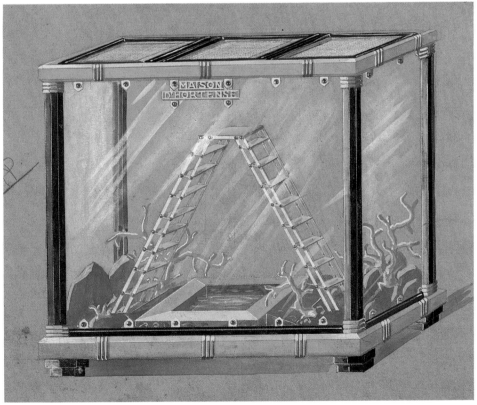

Birdcage in gold, onyx, lapis lazuli, grey agate, coral and cabochon rubies. Private collection, New York.

Aquarium, called the "Maison d'Hortense," made for a maharajah's tree frog, circa 1935. Private collection, New York.

Table night light in gold, rock crystal and green and black enamel, with ruby cabochons on the base. The light passes through the rock crystal, 1931. Van Cleef & Arpels collection.

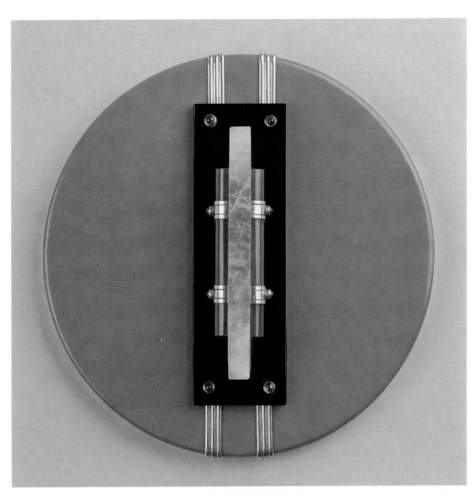

Mirror-back in green and black enamel, rose quartz, green agate, ruby cabochons and gold, 1930. Private collection, New York.

Mirror-back in black and red lacquer, agate, ruby cabochons and gold, 1930. Van Cleef & Arpels collection.

Window display in the Place Vendôme designed by François Canavy for Christmas 1979, on a symbolist theme: included are a portrait of a woman in the style of Knopff, an enamelled painting by Delaroche after a drawing by Gustave Moreau, and a corsage which had belonged to Madame Eiffel. Among the jewelry displayed are the sumptuous "Gazelle" necklace in rubies and diamonds and the "Double feather" clip in serti invisible *diamonds and rubies.*

Window display in the Place Vendôme designed by François Canavy for Christmas 1979, on a symbolist theme: an exceptional collection of emeralds is arranged around a statuette by Théodore Rivière.

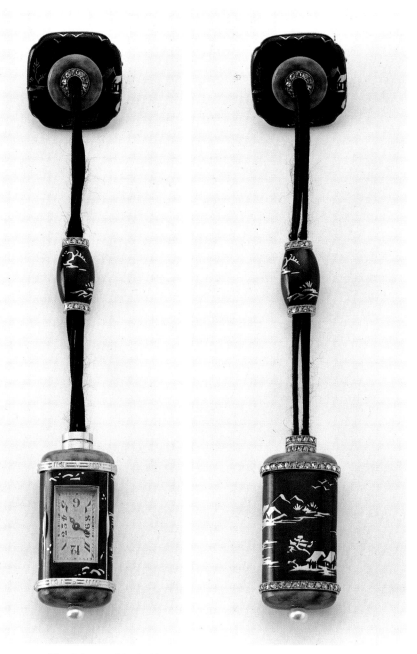

Châtelaine watch in the Chinese style of jade, black lacquer, pearl and diamonds, mounted on platinum, 1924. Enlargement. Van Cleef & Arpels collection.

Facing page: Châtelaine watch in coral, onyx and brilliants mounted on platinum, with matching pendant earrings, circa 1922. Private collection, Paris.

Page from a catalogue showing ladies' bracelet watches in platinum, diamonds and colored precious stones; the straps of some models are in black moiré or grosgrain, 1924–1925.

WATCHES

As the watch became an essential accessory during the twenties, Van Cleef & Arpels used all their imagination and ingenuity to transform this object into the most luxurious piece of jewelry: as a result, the fate of the watch became more and more closely linked with the jeweler's art. At the end of the twenties, pendant, châtelaine or "*Régence*" watches were being supplanted gradually by the bracelet watch, which was considered more functional. It became a precious object to the extent that it was worn with evening dress, in conjunction with other bracelets. Accordingly, the watch case was clothed in precious stones and the dial was sometimes hidden by a jeweled motif. The following few examples, made throughout the thirties and up until the fifties, were executed with numerous variations: the *à volets* (shutter) watch, on a bracelet of sapphires or rubies in *serti invisible*, was adorned on both sides by two discs of baguette diamonds (there was a more simple version in gold); the "Marguerite" clip in gold and colored precious stones could be attached to a gold serpent-chain, the center of the flower concealing the dial; in 1947, a "Diabolo" bracelet, formed of minute pyramids in relief, bore a scroll in gold scattered with small brilliants in which the dial was concealed. Certain women did not want to wear bracelet watches and for them the designers devised little watches which hooked onto the solid frame of bags made in leather or some precious fabric: one of the most original models, created at the beginning of the thirties, was executed using numerous different combinations of materials—yellow gold, grey gold, black enamel, coral—taking as its inspiration the car radiator. When the winder was gently rotated, little shutters opened and closed to reveal or conceal the dial.

Then the famous 'padlock' watch arrived on the scene, in gold and sometimes *calibré* precious stones, so popular with the female clientèle that it remained in the collections until the beginning of the sixties. Throughout the forties and fifties, ladies' bracelet watches would sometimes be embellished with motifs from the jewelry col-

Lady's bracelet watch in gold with the watch-case, embellished on both sides by six gold beads, attached to a strap composed of articulated, expandable gold plates, 1946.

lections, such as woven gold to imitate basketwork or braid, *guilloché* or chased gold. From the vast diversity of the collections, we might pick out those models created in 1953, composed of little leaves in gold and brilliants, or *faggots* in gold bound with a cord threaded through loops set with brilliants. In the fifties, precious wood was once again combined with gold in bracelet watches, for both men and women: these were reintroduced in the seventies.

Very often, throughout the twenties and thirties, men preferred to carry fob-watches: these were often adorned with geometric patterns or figurative designs, sometimes with a Chinese inspiration. For example, on the dial of a model from 1927, in grey gold with fillets of green gold, a Chinese magician was seated (in gold, enamel and colored precious stones) with articulated arms which, when a button-stem was pressed, rose to indicate the time. As for bracelet watches, a model from 1930, made up of several coins with a twenty dollar piece as its dial, achieved such success that it became a classic. Made also from ten dollar or hundred franc gold pieces, it competed later with another model, created in 1948, which was worn on a bracelet composed of gold *briquettes* which was threaded under the dial. Some years later, dials in *guilloché* gold or 'barley grain' gold, were placed in convex rectangular watch cases which were fluted at the side.

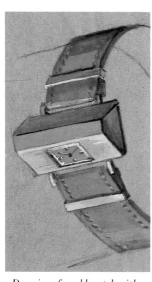

Drawing of a gold watch with a leather strap, made at the end of the thirties.

The House's most famous watch dates from 1949 and was to have an extraordinary destiny: this was the "P.A. 49" watch. Pierre Arpels wanted a unique watch, specially made for him. He took the purest geometric lines as his point of departure—the straight line and the circle—and conceived of an absolutely flat round watch case, attached by a delicate metal stud to a slender tangential *barrette*; two other studs, also spherical, extended from the extremities of the *barrette* which was covered by the leather strap so that only the three little gold beads were visible. The apparent fragility, the simplicity and the elegance of the watch were such that it immediately became a precious object that many people wished to possess and, indeed, when Van Cleef & Arpels opened their "Boutique des Heures" in

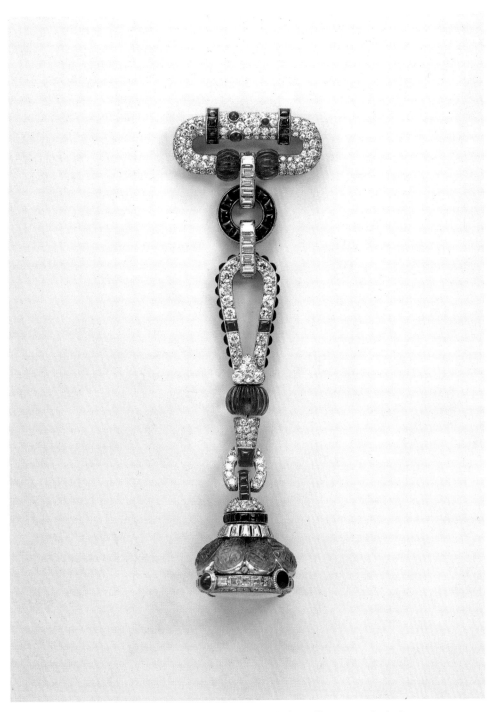

*Art Deco châtelaine watch with diamonds, cabochon rubies, engraved cabochon
emeralds*, calibré *sapphires and brilliants, 1928. Enlargement.*

1972, this watch occupied pride of place. All sorts of variations were devised from this model. During the seventies, sophisticated watches were very much in fashion. While always retaining the famous central fastening, the creators revived the skeleton watch whose mechanism was visible within the watch case, which was of gold and often set with brilliants or colored precious stones. There were also 'perpetual calendar' watches for which lapis lazuli was used to illustrate the phases of the moon and the cases and dials were made in mother-of-pearl, ebony, slate or tortoise-shell.

'Shutter' watch with strap in calibré *diamonds and two discs in baguette diamonds, one on either side of the watch-case, 1939.*

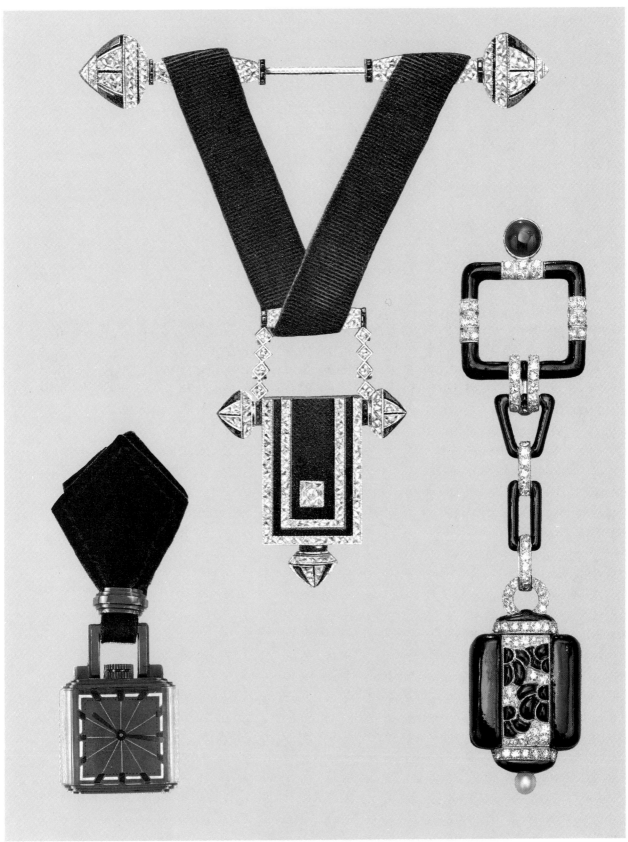

Pendant watch in gold and white enamel with a ribbon, 1936.

"Régence" watch in diamonds and onyx on platinum, hung from a black grosgrain ribbon attached to a matching bayonet pin, 1922.

Châtelaine watch with brilliants, onyx, jade and pearl winder, 1924. Private collection.

"Ludo" *bracelet watch: the strap is made up of slender rows of*
rectangular polished gold plates arranged like bricks in a wall,
with two flowers in yellow and blue faceted sapphires; the watch is
concealed in the center of one of these; the barrette-clasp is in
calibré *sapphires, 1946. Enlargement. Private collection, Paris.*
Photograph by Laurent Sully Jaulmes.

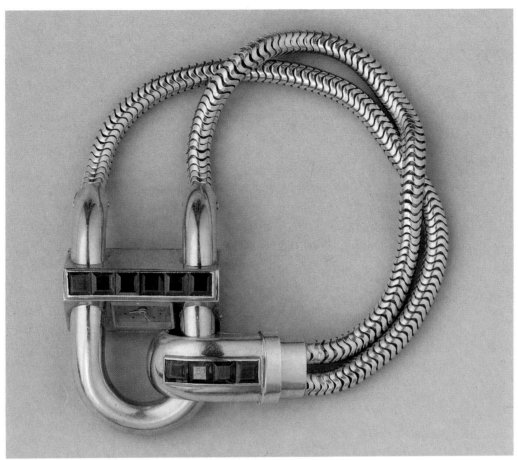

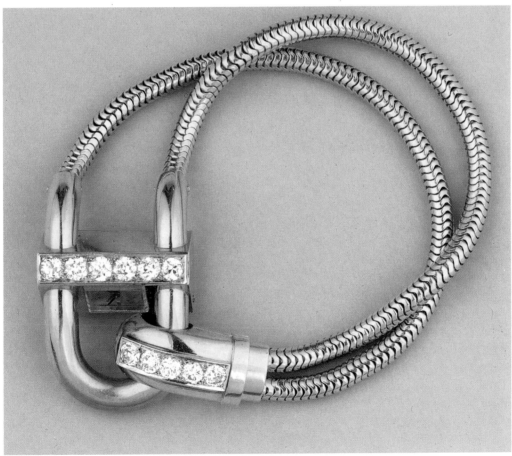

"Cadénas" (padlock) bracelet watch in polished gold with a line of calibré *sapphires and a serpent chain in gold, 1936. Private collection, Paris. Photograph by Laurent Sully Jaulmes.*

"Cadénas" bracelet watch in polished gold with a line of diamonds and a serpent chain, 1935. Private collection, Paris. Photograph by Laurent Sully Jaulmes.

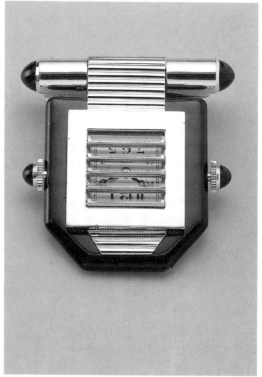

'Shutter' watch inspired by limousine radiators, in black lacquer
on a silver ground, gold and grey gold, shown open and closed,
1931. Van Cleef & Arpels collection.

Bag in red morocco, the clasp being adorned with a watch similar
to that shown above. Private collection, Paris.

Top left: Fob watch in white gold, crystal and enamel, 1928. Private collection, New York. Photograph by Michael Breskin Studio, New York.

Top right: Fob watch in grey gold called the "Bras en l'air" (arms in the air) or "Buddha" model. He occupies two thirds of the dial and indicates the time with his hands, 1927. Enlargement. Van Cleef & Arpels collection.

Bottom: Drawer-watch in precious wood, 1935. Van Cleef & Arpels collection.

"Skeleton" watch with the rim in gold, brilliants and rubies surrounding a dial
revealing the mechanical movement, and attached to the strap with gold set with
brilliants. The black satin strap has a buckle clasp which folds out, in gold set with
brilliants and rubies. It was created in 1980.

Facing page: The "P.A. 49" watch created in 1949 by Pierre Arpels; he conceived of a
round, flat watch-case, attached to a slender tangential barrette by a delicate metal
stud; two other spherical studs extend the extremities of the barrette which the leather
strap covers so that only the three gold beads appear. This watch inspired the creation of a
whole range of models distributed in the main capitals of the world under the term "The
Collection of Van Cleef & Arpels."

LARGE AND SMALL CLOCKS

Van Cleef & Arpels' creators brought all their subtlety to bear on the decoration of desk clocks and traveling clocks, which had been the exclusive province of clockmakers. They collaborated with the Verger workshop which at that time and throughout the twenties had no equal with regard to its spectacular 'mystery' clocks, the very symbol of the clock-as-jewel, which indicated hours and minutes only to royalty and the most eminent persons. These extraordinary clocks, whose hands seemed to float in space without any apparent connection with the movement, held a secret: each hand was imprisoned in a rock crystal disc with a notched metal rim, activated by a system of cogs hidden in the base or the frame of the clock case. One of the most extraordinary of these was a jade bear with an emerald eye, lying on his back on a pyramidal base of black onyx, supporting on his paws a crystal ball edged with black lacquer, the numerals and hands being set with rose-cut diamonds.

Another clock took the form of a Japanese temple portico: two columns of satin-finished crystal supported a gold cross-bar from which the irregular octagonal onyx clock case was suspended. The satin-finished crystal dial was sculpted in bas-relief with floral motifs, the numerals were replaced by the twelve signs of the zodiac painted in enamel on a black background, imitating the agate cameos of antiquity, surrounded on three sides by a row of diamonds, which were also used to decorate the hands. On 10 May 1979, at Christie's in Geneva, this model achieved the record price at auction for a timepiece: one million six hundred and ninety thousand francs.

Smaller portable clocks were often made in the form of a small cupboard—ideal for a traveling clock—as for example a model of 1926 in red lacquer, on which Chinese symbolic signs in black enamel formed hinges and catch, with a grey agate base.

Van Cleef & Arpels used all their powers of invention to vary the form of the dial, the hands and the numerals: floral compositions invaded the dials, as in that model of 1927 where the black lacquer clock case framed a lapis dial encrusted with turquoise flowers with opal centers and jade leaves. A variation was made in coral, onyx, jade and engraved crystal. The hands were often elaborately worked or chased, like little works of art and might on occasion become diamond-studded serpents, precious flowers, or Chinese characters. Oriental influence can be detected in numerous models: sculpted figurines or animals in ivory or hard stones were often used (the dog of Fo, buddhas, billikens, netsuke). On the other hand, we should mention a clock of 1928, completely free from oriental influence and utterly original: on a black onyx base with a geometric motif in diamonds at each extremity, a translucent crystal dial, in the form of a protractor marked out with hours and minutes, was attached to a satin-finished crystal motif in bas-relief depicting a fountain with jets of water spurting from it; the hand, reduced to a dot, was a triangular diamond which followed the curve of the semi-circular dial. Another one was made in the form of a pyramid in lapis and onyx, embellished with gold, sapphires and rubies, which supported a grey agate fountain basin on which two birds in lapis, jade and rubies perched; one of the birds, apparently quenching its thirst, indicates the hour with its beak on a dial whose diamond numerals are embedded in the basin.

Treated in a naturalistic style, popular jewelry motifs, borrowed from fauna and flora, were also used to embellish *pendules* and *pendulettes* of the forties and fifties. For example, a model of 1938 was inspired by the celebrated "Hawaii" motif: little birds in gold and precious stones are perched on branches at the foot of a small clock whose circular clock case is crowned with bouquets of flowers in brilliants and rubies (one of these clocks was acquired by Princess Fawzia of Egypt). In the same naturalistic spirit, a small clock was made in 1951, whose circular clock case was placed on an engraved base embellished with bunches of daisies in yellow gold, faceted and *calibré* emeralds, surrounded by a dial engraved with flowers. This model was revived in 1955, leaves of gold set with rubies replacing

Clock in the form of a Japanese temple portico created in 1926: two satin-finished crystal columns support a gold cross bar from which hangs an irregular octagonal clock-case in onyx. The satin-finished crystal dial is sculpted in bas-relief with floral motifs; the numerals have been replaced by the twelve signs of the zodiac painted in enamel on a black ground, imitating the agate cameos of antiquity, and framed on three sides by a line of diamonds which also embellish the hands. On 10 May 1979, at Christie's in Geneva, it achieved the world record for a time-piece at an auction sale, reaching 1,690,000 francs. Van Cleef & Arpels collection.

"Mystery" clock: a jade bear with an emerald eye, lying on its back on a pyramid-shaped base in black onyx, supports on its paws a crystal disc edged with black lacquer, the numerals and hands—in the Chinese style— are set with rose-cut diamonds.

the flowers. A small traveling clock, simple and functional in design, became one of Van Cleef & Arpels' unrivaled classic creations: hidden in a miniature flat box with a drawer or sliding panel, it was to be successively executed in a range of different materials; *guilloché* or 'barley grain' gold, woven gold imitating basketwork, *amourette* wood, and even black plexiglass. It disappeared from the collections but, in 1980, it was reintroduced with great success. Small clocks were sometimes disguised in a shell of woven gold, or in a ladybird's carapace. We ought also to mention a small clock made in 1966 whose clock-case was embellished with a fine ring of twisted gold and enclosed by a free-turning circle which formed a support, and the 'sun' model, where embossed yellow gold gave the illusion of a star radiating light.

These examples testify to Van Cleef & Arpels' skill in raising the accessory to the rank of precious object and even work of art. As Jacques Arpels was wont to say over the years, their vocation "was not necessarily to be the biggest, but always the best."

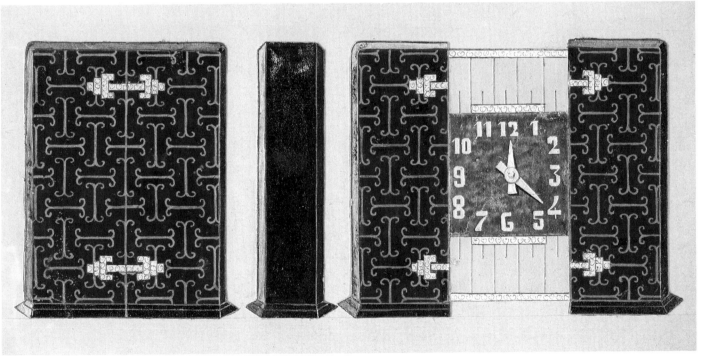

Clock inspired by Japan, in red enamel, agate and gold; the dial is in engraved jade, edged with a line of rose-cut diamonds, as are the clasps of the doors of the chest. The back of the clock depicts a Japanese landscape, 1930.

Clock with a pyramid-shaped base in lapis and onyx, embellished with gold, sapphires and rubies, which supports a grey agate fountain basin on which two birds in lapis, jade and rubies perch; the bird who seems to be drinking indicates the time with its beak on a dial with diamond numerals set in the basin, 1928.

Clock with a circular dial in engraved gold fixed to a base of gold branches on which perch three little birds in gold and precious stones apparently looking at the dial. The clock-case is topped by small flowers in brilliants and rubies, 1948.

Clock with a circular dial in engraved gold fixed to a base of gold branches, with bunches of "Hawaii" flowers, and a bird, made in emeralds, rubies and brilliants, perched over the dial, 1950.

Art Deco clock in black lacquer: the dial is decorated with enamelled and engraved flowers in jade, onyx, coral and crystal and the hands, inspired by Chinese signs, are in brilliants on gold, 1926.

Art Deco clock in rock crystal, circa 1925.

ACKNOWLEDGMENTS

The editor would like first of all to express his gratitude to Mr. Jacques Arpels, who initiated this book devoted to the Van Cleef & Arpels dynasty.

In addition, he would like to thank Sylvie Raulet, François Canavy and Jacques Boulay, respectively author, iconographer and photographer of this work.

He wishes also to express his heartfelt thanks for the invaluable help which Mr. Jacques Arpels and Mr. Claude Arpels have given him in placing their own recollections and their archives at his disposal; also to Mr. Philippe Arpels; Mr. Armand Campignon; Mrs. Monique Celaudoux; Mr. Jean Champion; Miss Nadine Coleno; Mrs. Caroline Daumen; Mrs. Dominique Hourtoulle; Mr. René-Sim Lacaze; Mr. Max Pelegrin; Mr. Ferdinand Ripoll; and Miss Micheline Roussier for their valued collaboration.

He extends his gratitude to all those who have helped him to recreate the history of Van Cleef & Arpels and have allowed him access to certain documents or collections of exceptional jewelry: Mr. Jean Marie Aude; Mrs. Paule Autissier; Mr. Bob Bénamou; Miss Yvette Benoit; Miss Monique Bergé; Mrs. Marie-Thérèse Berti; Mr. Jean Pierre Brun; Miss Liliane Bunout; Miss Maria Bussman; Mr. Gérard Colbert; Mr. and Mrs. Bernard Danenberg, Louvre des Antiquaires, Paris; Mr. Jean-Pierre Demand, société Artgem; Mrs. Yvonne Deslandres, Union Française des Arts du Costume; Mrs. Danièle Diard; Mr. Jacques Dubois; Mr. Ralph Esmerian; Mrs. Melissa Gabardi; Mrs. Odette Gasnier; Miss Christine Gouet; Mr. Jacques Guillemaud; Mrs. Charlotte Green; Miss Daisy Haber, New York; Mrs. Isabelle d'Hauteville; Mrs. Sylviane Humair; Mrs. Ully Jalou, l'Officiel de la Couture; Mr. Michel Jardelot; the John Jesse and Irina Laski Gallery, London; Mrs. Marie-Andrée Jouve; the Lewis M. Kaplan Gallery, London; Mrs. Rose Marie Kenmore; Mrs. Odette Langlois; Mr. Fred Leighton, New York; Mr. Claude Lemarié; Mrs. Isabelle de Lencquesaing; Mr. Jacques Lenfant; Mrs. Christine Léon; Miss Isabelle Léonard; Mr. and Mrs. Alain Lesieutre; Mr. Yvan Le Tourneur; Mrs. Véronique Ma'arop; Mrs. Hélène Marcantoni; Mr. Félix Marcilhac; Mrs. Monique Maury; Mrs. Suzanne Moerh; Mrs. Liliane Mouchian; Maison Oxeda; Miss Isabelle Parvex; Mr. Michel Périnet; Mr. Bernard Péry; Mrs. Brigitte Péry Evenot; Miss Sylvia Pitoeff; Mr. and Mrs. J. Polack; Mr. Guy Poussard; the Primavera Gallery, New York; Mr. Francesco Proia; Mr. Jean-Pierre Quémard; Miss Aline Queffurus; Mr. Claude Renon, Edition Brunétoile; Mrs. Germaine Richard; Mr. Daniel Riche; Mr. Michel de Robert; Mrs. Hélène Rochas; Miss Monica Rott; Miss Françoise Rousseau; Mr. and Mrs. de Sahb; Mrs. Sophie Sandlarz; Mr. A. Schar, Antiquités Zervudachi; Mrs. Anne Scrive-Loyer; Mr. Max Simon; Mr. Michel Souillac; and everyone at the House of Van Cleef & Arpels, all of whom have willingly given their invaluable assistance.

He expresses heartfelt thanks also to Princess Jeanne-Marie de Broglie of Christie's Paris; Mr. Hans Nadelhoffer and Mr. Rolf Schwieger of Christie's Geneva; Mr. François Curiel, and Mrs. Patricia Ferenczi of Christie's New York; Mr. Albert Middlemiss of Christie's London; Mrs. Marie-Odile Deutsch of Sotheby's Paris; Mr. Bernard Berger and Mr. Nicolas Rayner of Sotheby's Geneva; Mrs. Brigitte Blangey of Sotheby's Zurich; Mr. John Block of Sotheby's New York; Mr. Philippe Garner and Mr. Graham Llewellyn of Sotheby's London.

Photographs courtesy of: Agip Agency; Cecil Beaton; Mr. Roland Bianchini; the Michael Breskin Studio, New York; Mr. Jacques Boulay; Gamma Agency; Keystone Agency; Mr. Pierre Leclerc; Mr. Robert Lorenzson, New York; Mr. Roger Schall; Mr. Riad Shfhata; Mr. Laurent Sully Jaulmes; Mr. Jean Michel Tardy; Mr. André Thévenet; Mr. Dan Torrès; Mr. Trossey; Mr. François Vannereau.

INDEX